The Cult of the Tiger

The Cult of the Tiger

VALMIK THAPAR

OXFORD
UNIVERSITY PRESS

OXFORD
UNIVERSITY PRESS

YMCA Library Building, Jai Singh Road, New Delhi 110 001

Oxford University Press is a department of the University of Oxford. It furthers the
University's objective of excellence in research, scholarship, and education
by publishing worldwide in

Oxford   New York

Auckland Bangkok Buenos Aires Cape Town   Chennai
Dar es Salaam Delhi Hong Kong Istanbul Karachi Kolkata
Kuala Lumpur Madrid Melbourne Mexico City Mumbai Nairobi
São Paulo Shanghai Taipei Tokyo Toronto

Oxford is a registered trademark of Oxford University Press
in the UK and in certain other countries

Published in India
By Oxford University Press, New Delhi

First published 2002
Second impression 2004

ISBN 019 566036 6

Typeset in Lapidary 12/14
by Eleven Arts, Keshav Puram, Delhi 110 035
Printed in India by Pauls Press, New Delhi 110 020
Published by Manzar Khan, Oxford University Press
YMCA Library Building, Jai Singh Road, New Delhi 110 001

To my son
Hamir
&
to all those who
worship the ground
on which the tiger walks

Author's Note

This is a very special book for me. It connects my university days in Delhi with the tiger. Twenty years after graduating in social anthropology, I ended up researching the symbolism around the tiger and finally a decade later, comes this small book on 'the soul of Asia'—the tiger.

The tiger mesmerized, frightened and inspired all the human beings in its range. Even though this range has been sharply reduced, the tiger still continues to inspire all kinds of people around it. This book is about its all-powerful cult.

I have to thank the superb library at the School of Oriental and African Studies in London for providing me with a tiny glimpse into a wealth of information. I have to thank Priya Rana for all her work on this publication. Also my special thanks to Dr Romila Thapar for all her clues into the history of tiger belief. My final but most important thanks to Paola Manfredi for her inspiration to me over many years in the pursuit of the material for this book.

Valmik Thapar

x   Contents

List of Illustrations

All the illustrations are facing those pages listed.

Introduction

The Asian tiger today is an endangered species. Until very recently, the entire continent from the cold Siberian forests of Eurasia down to the lush tropical forest of Indonesia formed its stronghold, where it roamed majestically and fearlessly, sharing the land not only with a wealthy fauna but also with forest communities among which it enjoyed a sacred status.

Why sacred? I think that all those people who lived in the world of the tiger and who saw it and sensed it, were totally mesmerized by its presence. In the thick forests, the tiger would suddenly appear and then disappear. It created an illusory feeling and most human beings found ways to respect the tiger because of its impact upon them. Fear creates respect. The tiger was the most powerful predator that walked the earth!

When I saw it for the first time as a 'city person' in the forest, the tiger made an enormous impression on me. I remember writing about my first encounter: 'At last I saw it! The unmistakable glow of the striped coat and the powerful, unhurried, silent walk—this was my first tiger strolling confidently down the middle of the road. The power and sheer beauty of that moment cast a spell which was to become a driving passion in my life in the months and years ahead.' Twenty-six years after that day, the tiger's spell envelops me as much as it did forest communities in the land of the tiger. This book is about the impact of this spell on human beings.

This book traces the interface between man and tiger from the glacial Siberian wilds to the whole of Asia where the tiger had such a hold over the entire area that it spread through legend, myth, and ritual. It is notable that among all the communities that shared the forest with the tiger, it was never feared as a bloodthirsty, mindless killer; rather it enjoyed a sacred 'protected status', as protector of the forests. Never was the tiger wantonly killed, and elaborate codes guarded all game for the people who greatly depended on it for their livelihood. Even with the early advent of trophy-hunting, wantonly-killing Europeans, anyone who transgressed these codes by acting as tiger guides to the Europeans faced excommunication. It is only with the slow dying out of traditional ways of life of the forest people in the face of the relentless march of civilization that the tiger faced a threat.

Origins

The origin of the big cats is a subject of much debate. But the group as a whole is descended from the miacids, small insect-eating mammals that flourished more than 50 million years ago. Sabre-toothed cats in-

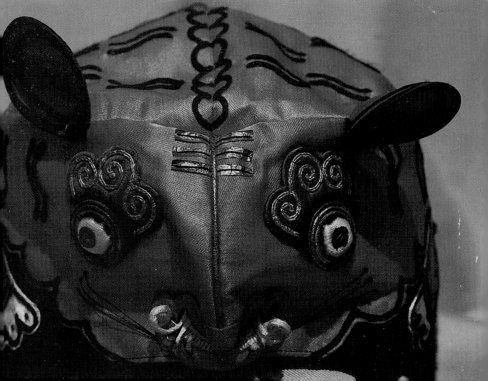

cluding the tiger appear in fossil records of Eurasia nearly 40 million years ago.

Large cats including tigers have evolved from a common ancestor probably similar to modern-day leopards or jaguars, 5 million years ago. The first fossils that can clearly be identified as tigers are nearly 2 million years old. Fossils found are primarily from Central Asia, Eastern and Northern China, Siberia, Japan, Sumatra and Java. It is clear that they were found not only in the forests of temperate and tropical Asia but in mangroves, scrub and thorn forests, and tall grass tracts on the flood plains of rivers. As far as we know the tiger is *solely Asian*.

The tiger has remarkable tolerance for the harsh climates of China and Siberia, Laos, Cambodia, Malaysia, Thailand, Indonesia, India, Nepal, Bangladesh, Bhutan, and Burma (Myanmar). Out of the eight sub-species, the Caspian, Javan and Bali are today extinct. There have been no tigers in Japan for thousands of years. There could be a handful of 10–15 tigers left in Korea. Iran lost its last tigers in the 1970s. But over thousands of years the impact of the tiger across Asia has been deep and powerful on all the people of this region. In a way, the tiger was the soul of Asia.

The People and their Tiger

It must have been like a bolt of lightning from the sky whenever forest dwellers across Asia caught a fleeting glimpse of the tiger, especially on moonlit nights, at dusk or at dawn. These were rare events, and the magic of the stripes seems to have been deeply embedded into the soul of Asia. For these forest dwellers, the link between man and tiger took on a spiritual dimension of its own—it came from close contact between humans and animals and from a belief that however different humans and animals are, they have similar souls.

Souls create and shape dreams and visions; they are much stronger than any individual's will. Most living things were regarded as having souls which were like a life force separate from the host body—the soul is the difference between a living body and a dead one. Anything living can be connected by the soul or be soul brothers; souls are mobile and can travel from one body to another. People and animals can therefore exchange souls, and this can take place while a human is alive or when he is dead. It is this belief in souls and their power that affected the behaviour of people towards animals in the forest, creating fear, awe, respect and in some cases worship. Animals, for so many families and communities, took on the form of totems and became objects to protect and respect. Because the tigers appeared and disappeared in the middle of the night, and they had the power and ability as predators to stalk, kill and be the kings of the jungle, they were frequently and commonly associated with soul transfers. The power and beauty of the tiger lent itself to this belief like no other and even where tigers killed and ate man, people believed that the soul of the person eaten by a tiger becomes the soul of the tiger—rarely was a man-eating tiger harmed. This was very different from modern Christian belief that attributed soulhood only to human beings. Henry Bandesson who studied the hill tribes of Vietnam reveals how in one case when a tiger killed a woman, it was thought to be inhabited by the soul of a deceived husband and a wave of marital fidelity swept through the village!

Bandesson also recorded that the soul of a tiger's victim is forced to ride its back, and maybe because of this remarkable association, tigers from Siberia, China, Indo-China, South-East Asia and India are depicted as being a vehicle on which human figures of goddesses like Durga, Daoist Popes in China, Tibetan goddesses, tribal gods and so much more ride on. In Indo-China, hunters of the tiger would even go to the extent of sprinkling roasted maize around a tiger trap to ensure that its human spirit smelt the grain and escaped from the trap!

Many forest dwellers were certain that tigers with human souls were eternal friends of people and therefore must never be harmed. These tigers with human souls protected people from danger and were always around in times of crisis. It is also how across Asia, shamans (individuals who use their special magical powers in a trance to associate with the spirit world) provide cures. In the land of the tiger the closest associates of the shamans were tigers themselves, and in his trance the shaman was transformed into a tiger to become the healer.

It is the spirit of the tiger that is called and if it appears, it bestows the power on the shaman to communicate with the spirit world. Anthropologist Richard Winstedt recorded,

a magician at a séance will growl and sniff and crawl under the mats and lick the naked body of the patient. His growls and movements showing that he has been transformed and so far from being possessed by his spirit he has obtained control of it. During a séance it is alleged, a tiger appears at least once, though experts debate whether it is a real animal or a were-tiger.

Winstedt also recorded that the corpse of a shaman is placed on a tree rather than buried 'so that he might turn into a were-tiger or so that his tiger spirit might visit him and release his soul, or desert his body for that of his successor'. Sometimes trees were very special to forest dwellers like the Mnong community in Indo-China. A scientific survey required the cutting down of a tree. The chief of the Mnong 'coolies' employed to help the scientists, approached the tree and addressed it with these words:

Spirit who last made thy home in this tree, we worship thee and come to claim thy mercy. The White mandarin, our relentless master, whose commands we cannot but obey, has bidden us to cut down thy habitation, a task that fills us with sadness and which we only carry out with regret. I adjure thee to depart at once from the place and seek a new dwelling place elsewhere, and I pray thee to forget the wrong we do thee, for we are not our own masters.

This speech was accompanied by complete obeisance and concluded by another to the king of the forest, the tiger, who has jurisdiction over each tree in the area. The Mnong believe that the tiger is first among animals and has great supernatural powers. They refer to him with respect and fear, calling him 'king of the mountain', 'his eminence', 'my lord', 'the gentleman', 'the master' or 'lofty one', rather than use the word 'tiger'.

It is this concept of fear and respect for the tiger that was found everywhere the tiger roamed. The cult around the tiger was and still is deeply rooted into the lives of those millions of people who live in and around Asia's tigers' forests. The tiger for most forest communities was a 'God-like figure'.

I have always been intrigued by the cult of the tiger and its symbolism. When I got the opportunity to spend six weeks in the superb library of the School of Oriental and African Studies in London, I jumped at the chance, and found endless connections between people and tigers. This book is a result of that research. I believe that much more needs to be done in this sphere. I am also convinced that one of the only reasons that the tiger is alive today is because of the power of its cult. This power was and still is a deterrent to those wanting to destroy the animal. Even today, on India's west coast near Mangalore, people paint themselves like tigers and dance each Dussehra to propitiate the Tiger God.

I hope that this book adds to the awareness of this powerful predator and increases the will to save it from extinction. In a way the tiger's cult has been its protective cloak and even though traditional beliefs have changed drastically in the last decade, I keep my fingers crossed that belief in the tiger will ensure its survival into the future.

2002   VALMIK THAPAR

The Cult of the Tiger

Siberia: The Land of Origin

Somewhere in Siberia millions of years ago, a flow of molten lava from the depths of the earth formed a crater for what is now a non-existent volcano. Slowly over time it cracked and congealed to form a multitude of boulders. The first descriptions of this stunning landscape come from travellers in the last couple of hundred years:

Rugged mountain jaws opened upon us in all their grandeur. This was a terrific rent: the dark purple slaty rock had been driven asunder by granite, and heaved up into craggy precipices of enormous height. In some parts the rocks were broken into sharp points; in others they were piled up like huge towers, overhanging the base of these mighty cliffs.

Opposite to one of the large islands are the high volcanic cliffs of Saen-doo; they jut far into the river, and stand out of the water like gigantic castles, quite in keeping with the vast flood at their feet. Several miles beyond this, is another volcanic mass, Mo-dad-Ze, a picturesque group of rocks rising to a great height, with deep recesses at intervals, which give the appearance of towers; and pinnacles, that when viewed at a distance, assume the character of an enormous Gothic structure.

This part of the Amoor, for a space of from forty to fifty miles, is not surpassed by any river scenery. Its great breadth, the numerous islands that seem floating on its surface, and high cliffs that rise out of its bed, produce a series of grand and constantly changing scenes. Oak-se-me is one of the last; it stands at the lower end of this vast line of crags, rising like a wall from the water to the height of 150 feet, and extends more than a mile in length. Deep ravines have been cut in the mass by torrents, which come tumbling down. They can only be heard, as groups of elm, ash and birch screen their falling streams, while the pine, aspen, and other trees crown the summit.

The exploration of these frozen lands was recent, as the area was cold, dark, and inaccessible. It led to a quiet discovery in the heart of Siberia giving some of the earliest information on the origins of the tiger—fossil remains of the Pleistocene sabre-toothed tiger found deep within the Chigar caves of the New Siberian Islands. This sabre-toothed tiger existed millions of years ago and became extinct only ten thousand years ago when its descendent, the true tiger, began to extend its range, moving southwards in search of more suitable habitats as successive phases of the ice ages made Northern Asia uninhabitable.

From the Tertiary period and over millions of years, specific fauna evolved that escaped the ice, descendents of pre-glacial fauna rather than survivors.

Today deep in the snow in the Russian Far East, two hundred tigers still roam. The area is the land of the Amur, a spectacular combination of plains and mountains, of the coast that faces the Sea of Japan, and of rivers like the Amur. The plains of the Ussuri stretch westwards from the Sikhote-Alin mountains, encompassing larch and conifer forests with large areas of marshland, and copses of dwarf pines on the summits. The area is home to a vast number of plant species including

species surviving from the Tertiary period which started 65 million
years ago.

Temperatures can go down to -35°C in this area, and the winter is
icy cold. But with the tiger, man also managed to survive, adjust to,
and live in what must be some of the most inhospitable natural
conditions found in the world. Man lived here, and still does, deeply
integrated with nature. The boulders on the banks of the Amur bear
witness to this age-old interface between man and nature.
Archaeologists in the 1930s discovered what is probably the first
representation by man of the tiger dating back to 4000–3500 BC,
etched on one of the boulders, surrounded by other boulders with
images of the elk, masked faces, and writhing snakes.

It was the distant ancestors of the Nanai, Oicha and Nivkh peoples
who shared this rugged terrain with the tiger and all of nature's cre-
ations. Early travellers in the nineteenth century discovered fascinating ethnographic information about these peoples and their
deep-rooted links with nature. Their writings refer to the Nanai by
the name 'Goldis'.

The Amoor becomes much narrower where it flows between the high
igneous shores, that extend a distance of nearly one hundred miles. Islands
are frequent even here, where the stream is more confined and numbers of
Goldi villages are found on both shores. The country is covered with forest
as far as the eye can reach. Tigers and panthers are very numerous, and
often visit the villages searching for prey.

Nature has been exceedingly bountiful in this region, and has bestowed on
the people some of her most valuable gifts. Magnificent forests contain timber
suited for every purpose, oak for shipbuilding, with elm, birch and pine for
domestic purposes. She has stocked these vast forests with many animals suited
for the food of man, while others produce furs of great value, for which he can
always find a market; and all multiply around him without giving him a moment's
care.

She has provided rich pastures for domestic animals, and the luxuriant
vegetation that springs up everywhere shows that man need only scatter

the seed into the earth, to ensure an abundant harvest, while the Amoor, and its effluents afford an inexhaustible supply of various kinds of fish.[1]

According to these early travellers, the Goldis chose the most picturesque sites for their dwellings, revealing great taste and judgement. Their huts were made of birch bark, effective in protecting them from sharp and diverse weather. They seem to have had a fascination for colour, and an early traveller states, 'The inhabitants of the Amoor paint all their household goods and portions of their dwellings with the most vivid tints; and, like the Chinese possess an excellent knowledge of the harmony of colours.'

The Goldis had Mongolian features and depended on fish. In this harsh climate there was a brief summer when large quantities of fish were caught and dried for use in the winter. This dried fish was ground like flour into fish cakes or 'yukola', a vital protein for man and animal in the winter when most supplies were exhausted. Today little has changed. Fish is still the staple food. But fish is not only a source of food. Fish skin is used to mend houses, and make clothing. Dried fish skin is crumpled into a ball, rolled and pounded in a wooden mortar, and when supple it is sewn together making trousers and shoes, the soles of the latter reinforced by reindeer hide. The men seem to use garments made of salmon skin, women choosing fish skin of pretty stripes and colours. Europeans referred to the Goldis as 'Fish-skin Tartars'.

Whether girls or boys, children are special and babies are put in birch bark cradles, padded with moss and shavings, suspended from the roofs of the huts. Dangling over the cradle to amuse the child, and rattling as the cradle swings, are strings of teeth and claws of various wild animals. When an infant is a few months old it is given a fish head to suck and cut its teeth upon, and in a little while it is ready for its first suit of fish skin clothes.

Reindeer and bear skins keep the Goldis warm in the winter. The flesh of the elk provides food, the bones are made into spears and arrowheads, and the antlers into bows. In their own words,

A Nanai [Goldi] lives in the forest, sleeps on the earth, lets the moon warm his back and fears neither heat nor cold. A long span of life is his potion. His eyes are very keen and his hearing is acute. He can even smell wild animals. Yes, he scents them out. Just you ask him!

They seem to have a fine memory of the forest and are able to retrace their steps even weeks later in endless, trackless forests. They have always had their own strict regulations for hunting which preserved the game, and rules in terms of hunting encampments and time spent in hunting are scrupulously observed. They tend to hunt alone. When fishing they worship the spirit of the water. The entire life of these people is dependent on success in fishing. In spring and autumn special food is cooked in wooden pans and dropped into the water. These are offerings to the spirit of the water, 'Yemu', the sea god.

When entering the forest they seek the favour of 'Anduri', the supreme, and propitiate 'Kamtchanga' the forest god with a gift of fishmeal cakes. The hunt is mainly for sable skins though animals like the fox and the musk deer are also killed. Men are mostly engaged in hunting between September and May. But ritual procedures are carefully observed and hunters treat even their kills with honour.

They revere the tiger and the bear as their sacred ancestors. The tiger was called 'amba' and never hunted in the past as it was considered protector and guardian of the forest. Even when the tiger sometimes raided hunters' snares for trapped deer, or carried their dogs off, or even ate their vital supplies of frozen fish, it was immediately forgiven. Anyone who killed a tiger was expelled from the tribe.

The Goldi religion is a mixture of totems, nature worship, and fetishism. The shaman priesthood is the intermediary between the living and the supernatural world. They perform a variety of duties from curing the sick to making sacrifices and ministering on occasions of misfortune and death by conducting prayers; they are soothsayers, battle with evil spirits, and even perform magic. The shamans bedeck themselves in fur robes, the bones and teeth of sea animals, and metal images of birds and beasts, giving them a man–animal look. A shaman describes how he got prompted into shamanism:

Once I was asleep on my sick bed, when a spirit approached me. It was a very beautiful woman.

She said, 'I am the "ayami" of your ancestors, the shamans. I taught them shamaning. Now I am going to teach you. The old shamans have died off, and there is no one to heal people. You are to become a shaman.'

Next she said, 'I love you, I have no husband now, you will be my husband now and I shall be a wife unto you. I shall give you assistant spirits. You are to heal with their aid, and I shall teach and help you myself.'

Sometimes she comes as a winged tiger. I mount it and she takes me to show me different countries. I have seen mountains, where only old men and women live, and villages, where you see nothing but young people, men and women: they look like Goldis and speak Goldish. Sometimes those people are turned into tigers. Now my ayami does not come to me as frequently as before. Formerly, when teaching me, she used to come every night. She has given me three assistants—the jarga [the panther], the doonta [the bear] and the amba [the tiger]. They come to me in my dreams and appear whenever I summon them while shamaning.[2]

The invocation of the tiger spirit by the shaman was a vital facet in the religion of the Goldi or Nanai. In a way, their rhythm of life was enmeshed with the tiger and the forest.

A very special Nanai ritual related to the bear. Once a year a young bear was caught and slowly fattened for the 'bear feast' held in mid-winter. This was probably an expression of gratitude for success in hunting. A few decades ago a film crew tried to capture this ritual on camera by recreating it but the Nivkh people declined to compromise on the ritual significance and felt that it would be a sin to kill a bear not specifically nurtured by them for the purpose. This is an insight into traditional sanctions on game.

Ceremonial dress worn on certain occasions reveal the infinite and deep-rooted significance and symbolism, of nature in Nanai life. Elks, birds, the sun, tigers, and snakes would be minutely embroidered into the branches of the 'tree of life' or the 'tree of the world', which was and still is the essence of all life.

But in the last few centuries the advent of the Europeans and outsiders seriously affected life in this area. Nanai people became victims of oppressive Russian law and tax collection on the one hand and Chinese liquor traders on the other. Both exploited them for furs and skins of animals, buying them at one-tenth of the price fixed. As greater numbers became addicted to intoxicating liquor, more and more animals had to be hunted and by the nineteenth century there was a decline in their numbers. With them the Nanai faded away slowly, their religion, ritual, and culture destroyed by outsiders. Wrote one traveller, 'In this and other ways the conditions of their life are becoming harder and more impractical every year, and in a few decades the race will be extinct.'

This was also the moment for the European hunter to make his entrance into the primeval forest. He came with guns, enticing local tribals to act as guides to 'scent out' animals, especially the tiger. Some voluntarily abandoned their traditional culture and others were expelled. The way of life along the Amur slowly changed.

From the European hunters came the first records of the Amur or Siberian tiger.

We thought he had found a herd, but on reaching him he pointed to the soft ground, covered with footprints and gore, where a terrible conflict had evidently taken place. At first we thought the bears had been fighting, but a closer inspection showed us that one had been measuring his strength with a more formidable foe—a tiger: whose footprints were stamped around the field of battle. The boar had been slain and carried off: it was easy to trace the crimson track, which led towards a mass of high reeds, into which the tiger had carried his prey. A well-trodden path or reedy tunnel formed the approach to his lair, which was about two feet six inches wide, and three feet and a half in height, thickly matted over into an arch. The tiger had put down his burden at the entrance of this covered way, the red marks being distinctly visible. The men thought the battle had been fought three or four days ago; from this they concluded that a tigress and her cubs were in their den not far off; and in confirmation of their opinion, the dogs barked furiously.[3]

Even the hunter with his gun on encountering the tiger always seemed at first paralysed. One says, 'I felt an unbearable weight on my shoulders as if someone was trying to push me into the earth.'

But there was also humour in some of these encounters. One example is that of a hunter riding back to town after successfully dispatching a tiger.

En route the tiger came to its senses, again, roared and began to tear at the rope with which it was tied to the sledge. The horse bolted. The old man sat paralysed with fear because he had not so much as an axe in the sledge to hit the tiger with. His terrified son ran behind the sledge but could not shoot; he might have hit his father or the horse instead of the tiger. So the father charged into the village with the roaring tiger.[4]

Much of the hunting in Siberia was done with the help of dogs that could pinpoint the tiger, chase it through sheets of snow, and circle it while the hunter followed slowly behind. Surrounded, the tiger would deal severe blows on many of the dogs with its paws but finally their sheer numbers would overwhelm it.

The tribal guides of these hunters expressed their wonder at the tiger's strength, since it took several bullets to kill it.

By the turn of the century, the tiger was fading from the Siberian forests. The fur trade in tiger skins and in those of its prey species had taken its toll.

The Amur tiger is one of the most remarkable of its species, weighing 350 kilos, 4 metres long, and able to withstand a harsh clime and deep snows. Its long warm coat and its layer of fat protect it from the cold. In the area of the Amur, the tiger seemed to have had a weakness for wolves, pursuing and killing them whenever encountered. It also hunted dogs, snatching them from hunting lodges or human settlements. Some say that it has also been known to tear a horse from its harness and carry it off into the jungle. Besides its diet of deer, the wild boar seems its favourite prey. Taiga dwellers call the Amur tiger the 'hog herdsman' as it herds and chases a group of boar till it picks on a young hog to kill. Seldom in this area has a tiger attacked old boars with their formidable tusks. There are few cases of the Amur tiger attacking and killing people except when cornered by hunters.

There is little information on the natural history of the tiger in this area. During the middle of this century there were about 100 tigers left in the Ussuri taiga. Today there may be 300. Their individual range can extend to 150 sq. km. They are now concentrated in the Primorye territory in the Sikhote-Alin and Lazovsky state reserves and its adjacent areas. It is today the only viable population of this sub-species.

The forms of religious belief amongst the Amur people have also faded with the tiger. Only a few people of the older generation retain some of the beliefs that integrated man, tiger, and the forest. This is reflected sometimes in an ancient art that has lived on even as the tiger disappeared. The future is bleak. The life of man and tiger under the umbrella of nature has been completely disrupted with the advent of 'modern civilization'. Somewhere we have to rediscover the roots that sustained a harmony between man and nature.

Into the Caspian

A land where legends of man, tiger, and nature abound: A princess waits on the bank of a river, desperate to cross to the other side. The waters of the river rage. Suddenly a tiger appears at her side. She gets on to his back and they set forth to cross the waters. The tiger is a powerful swimmer and carries the princess safely to the other side. The princess delivers a baby on the far bank. The river is called Tigris and weaves a long course in this land revealing the 'fertile connections' between man and tiger.

Sadly, however, the Caspian tiger is completely extinct and the only description of it in the wilds that I have uncovered is from Teheran in the middle of the last century:

Our young people started off in quest of a good spring of water for our tea; but all at once we heard a fearful cry of distress. They came flying back, and recounted to us that they had seen animals at the source, which sprang away with long bounds when they approached them. At first I thought they must be lions, and I seized a rusty sword, and found in the direction they had described, but at a good distance off, two splendid tigers, whose beautifully striped forms made themselves visible occasionally from the thickets.[5]

However, the tiger retains a special place in Islam, as is testified by its sacred central image on the carpets and textiles of the region.

The Caspian tiger seems to have centred itself around the Caspian and, as Carruthers put it in his book, *Beyond the Caspian*, 'A line drawn from the south of the Caspian sea straight across Middle Asia to Lop Nor in Chinese Turkestan, up north west to Balkhash and back again to Aral and the Caspian would enclose all the existing haunts of this species.'[6]

He went on to state that tigers had not been seen in the vicinity of Bukhara for the past fifty years but were still found around the Oxus where they endlessly predated on wild pigs in the marshes. He says,

But still they are not protected and are in danger of becoming extinct. Around Balkhash they are now very scarce; on the Syr they are gone for ever except as a rare visitor from the Oxus delta (Russian officers used to hunt them from Tashkent); their Dzungarian haunts were never very extensive, but, on the other hand, they are more remote and as yet undeveloped, so tigers may still survive there; the Hyrcanian forests on the northern slopes of Elburz, the Atrek region and the Murghab still hide a few; but the basin of the Oxus probably holds a larger population of Central Asian tigers than any other area at the present day. Chiefly relegated to the reed-beds around its many-mouthed delta, they occur spasmodically over the frontiers of Darwaz, right under the Pamirs. A line drawn across the river from Chubek to Chayab would mark their eastern limit.[7]

In all these habitats of the Caspian tiger, the local communities always held that the tiger harmed no one and there seemed to be a kind of balance between man and animal.

There have been no reliable reports of the Caspian tiger since the 1950s. Formerly, the Caspian tiger lived in the lowland forest and marshes bordering the Caspian Sea. Today, the lowlands have been converted to agricultural lands, which must have forced the tiger to retreat to the upper mountainous belts from where also it slowly vanished. Too much of its habitat had given way to agriculture and it was hunted out of its last refuges in the mountains.

The last credible report of the Caspian tiger dates to 1958 in the scrub forests of what is today the Mohammed Reza Shah National Park.

This sub-species may have slipped through from India to Pakistan into the land of the Caspian or spread from north-west Russia encompassing a belt that could have connected it to India.

In any case Afghanistan and Pakistan had tigers and the last tiger in Pakistan is supposed to have been shot at the turn of the century. The last stronghold of the tiger was the riverine forest along the Indus.

Into Korea

The tiger in Korea was a symbol of strength and courage and had a 'protected' status among forest communities. Tiger hunters in Korea found it exceedingly difficult to gather information on tigers from forest communities.

In vain did we offer, at length, extravagant prices for the beasts? Even fifty dollars, with the bones and carcass thrown in, for each tiger we shot, would not tempt them.

We also offered twenty-five dollars for a shot at a tiger, and ten dollars for the mere sight of one, but equally in vain. Although the people at Pochon strenuously denied the death of any one there from tigers, and even the very existence of these beasts, yet Mr Campbell, when he visited that village in 1889, was told that in the last year eighteen people had been killed by them.[8]

The forest communities of Korea were guarding their deep-rooted links with the tiger, protecting it against the pressures of hunters. But it was not to last long.

In Korea the white tiger occupied pride of place with the blue dragon as a symbol of auspiciousness and a repeller of evil. Blue dragon and white tiger paintings adorned most Korean homes. Sadly this art now lives only in the Emille Museum and some temples. A prime example is that of 'A Wicked Woodcutter Being Eaten by a Tiger in Hell', housed in the Hwa Jang Sa Temple, Seoul. It establishes the vital role of the tiger as protector of the forest.

Tiger skin screens were used in Korea to ward off evil. Real skins were highly prized for their magical powers to repel evil. Tradition

also dictated the draping of a tiger blanket on a bride's palanquin in a wedding procession. In the past, real skins were used, but in recent times a thick cloth painted with tiger stripes substituted to keep away evil influences from the bride, in order that the couple could be happy and have many children.

Koreans venerated tigers as the benevolent messengers of the mountain spirit, which was the most popular member of the shaman pantheon in Korea. Maybe a few Korean tigers still roam the mountainous regions of this land. San Shin or the mountain spirit is depicted in paintings as an old man with a white beard seated under a pine tree and accompanied by his messenger the tiger. He often holds a walking stick and a fan. There are thousands of San Shins all over Korea at sacred sites like the Diamond Mountains, or perched high on cliffs, and in many old homes.

The image of the tiger seems to 'watch over' the land of Korea, as guardian and protector. Korean folk literature and legend is rich with tales of the tiger. In one:

A young man was walking through the mountains beating a long drum. The mountains rang with the rhythm of the drum and the melody of his voice raised in song. Before long he saw a big yellow tiger come out of the forest and dance to his music. He was terrified at its appearance, and realised that he could not stop playing, for if he did the tiger would assuredly fall upon him and eat him up. So he went on playing to keep it in good humour, and walked backwards so that he could face it and watch what it might do.

Before long he came to a village. All the villagers were very amused to see him, with the tiger dancing before him. It seemed to be quite tame, for it attacked no one, and people began to throw money to the youngest son.

One of the (king's) daughters fell in love with him, and the king consented to their marriage. And so the youngest son became the husband of a Royal Princess, and the tiger was made a Royal pet.[9]

The Amur tiger slipped into Korea through Khabarovsk where it could be found till early this century. In his book *In Korean Wilds and Villages*, Sten Bergman narrates an encounter with a Russian hunter named

Jackovski in Korea who recalled his experiences of shooting tigers in Siberia. 'Yes,' he answered, 'several'.

The first I shot when I was seventeen. My brother Alexander and I were riding through the taiga one winter day. We were going along the side of a steep incline when suddenly our horses became uneasy. An instant later a powerful tiger came for us in a series of mighty leaps. We jumped off before he was too near and the tiger sprang upon one of the horses. Tiger and horse went tumbling down the slope. My brother and I both fired at the tiger, which was finally dispatched by a bullet of mine.

The Eastern Siberian tiger is unique in its beauty, with its long haired winter coat. Thirty years ago fifty or sixty tigers used to be shot every winter in the Vladivostok region, but now they have almost been exterminated.

In the Siberian forests there was plenty of game at that time. Apart from tigers, I used to go after wolves, bears, leopards, gorals and roe deer to say nothing of wild fowl, geese, ducks and pheasants and much else. But, in Korea, I have not had a chance of shooting a single tiger during all the thirteen years I have been here. I have sighted several, however, and I once captured two little tiger cubs. The tiger is almost exterminated here also.[10]

Sten Bergman goes on to state, 'In all the virgin forests which we were now traversing there were tigers, leopards, lynxes, bears and wild boar in addition to the deer.'

In his book entitled *Korea and the Sacred White Mountain,* A.E.T. Cavendish states of tigers, 'We afterwards learnt that the mountains between us and the sea swarmed with these beasts.'[11]

Part of the tribute paid to Japan for many years in Korea's history included forty tiger skins the hair of which was 'a finger long'. The tribute to China included a hundred tiger skins.

The use of the tiger's flesh, entrails, and bones seemed widespread in Korean medicine but in this century very rarely could a carcass be found since the tiger had been widely exterminated.

Even early this century there seemed a large movement of tigers from the mountains to the plains, especially in the winter. Tiger traps were regularly constructed to catch the roving tiger. In 1890, 7 leopard skins, 30 tiger skins, and 3 live tigers were exported by sea, and 67 tiger skins were exported from Chemulpho. But fur, hunting, and the erosion of the Korean forest in the last century have ended the Korean tiger's story.

The Tiger in Manchuria and China

The Amur or Siberian tiger also slipped into Manchuria where it was commonly known as the Manchurian tiger. A few tigers may also have disappeared into Mongolia, but there is no record from there, even though there have been references to the Mongolian tiger.

But the tiger flourished a few hundred years ago in northern and eastern Manchuria near the west bank of Ussuri River. In these communities hunting and fishing were vital with hoe agriculture sometimes alternating seasonally with hunting. Rivers like the Yalu and the Tumen were rich in fish. Some of these forest people used advanced techniques of reindeer domestication for milk and transport. Reindeer skin was used for most items of dress. 'Curried' reindeer skin was worn around the hips, the pelt of young reindeer fawn made up stockings, and old reindeer hide boots. The upper dress also came from the skins of young deer.

Manchuria's traditional and most important trade was in silk and with the coming of new traders, the fur trade boomed. This in turn took its toll on the traditions of the forest communities and on the tiger. Alexander Hosie states in his book, *Manchuria—Its People, Resources and Recent History,*

The mountains and forests of Manchuria, especially the Cha'ng-Pai Shan and Hsing—and ranges, in the Kirin and Hei Lung-chiang provinces respectively, are tenanted by bears, leopards, sables, squirrels and tigers, and the hunters who dwell in huts on the mountain valleys, are nominally under the jurisdiction of an official superintendent.[12]

Tributes were made of animals and furs to the emperor. Tigers were usually caught in large traps with pigs being used as bait. In the customs returns for 1896 in New-Chwang, tiger skins fetching £6 each have been listed and larger well-marked tiger skins could fetch upto £15 each. The Manchurian tiger skin was considered much finer than the Indian tiger skin.

Tiger bones, vital in Chinese medicine, were also sold in this year; 3600 lb of bones valued at 3 pence per lb were also exported. All this led to immense exploitation of the tiger which must till then have freely roamed the wooded parts of northern China. Even till 1923 Sowerby states that in Hopei it was still to be found near the Eastern Tombs and imperial hunting grounds to the north-east and north of Peking.

An early traveller states, 'While up hunting in the highest parts of the range, I came across tiger tracks in the snow. The Chinese in the district said that there were tigers but refused absolutely to lead me to their haunts, so greatly did they fear this animal.'[13] However, it was not fear but the tiger's sacred status as a vital element of their forests that was productive of this protective attitude towards it.

But in the twentieth century the tiger was nearly wiped out in this area. The Heilongjiang province in China had Siberian tigers in every mountainous area in the past. This was the Chinese side of the Amur River. In the early 1960s the forests of Yichun were said to be full of tigers.

In 1980 the Quixinglazi Nature Reserve was created to protect the few tigers left in this area. Here there are ancient forests of Korean pines on the banks of raging rivers. The most famous peak nearby on the Korean border is the White Head Mountain with the crater 'lake of heaven'. The mountain is considered sacred and is at the centre of the

Changbai Nature reserve, which sprawls over 2000 sq. km. About fifty surviving north-eastern China tigers or Siberian tigers share the area with snow leopards, sables, and bears, and the Oroquen who are traditional forest hunters. They are said to number 4000 and live in tents made of birch bark in the summer and deer skin in the winter. They hunt and raise reindeer. Their source of income is the deer, as the deer's embryo, antlers, penis, and tail are vital ingredients in Chinese medicine. The Oroquen eat meat, fish, and wild plants. Raw deer liver is a delicacy. They believe in spirits and shamans, and a shaman is supposed to turn into a tiger after his death. The concept of were-tiger exists among them. It is believed that men can take the form of tigers and tigers can take the form of men. Now with tigers and the forests vastly depleted, the traditional culture of these people is in conflict with the world around them.

From Manchuria the tiger passed into the rest of China, leaving its imprint everywhere. The relationship between man and tiger in China goes back a million years to the Pleistocene period as there are reports of tiger remains from the lower Pleistocene period in the Shansi province. China has been the home to four sub-species of the tiger and the most ancient tiger-like skull was found here and estimated to be over two million years old. Some believe that the tiger might have spread around the world from China.

The Yunan province in south-west China where the average altitude is 6500 feet, the landscape unspoilt, with bare mountains speckled here and there with green trees, calm rivers, and narrow valleys, is home to the Naxi people. The Naxi are said to have Tibetan origins and practise Bon, the ancient pre-Buddhist religion of Tibet. Their religion also has elements of Chinese shamanism, rife with astronomy, magic, and exorcism. There are still 30–40 practising Dongba shamans among them.

They invoke the tiger as a spirit, and the tiger occupies a central place in their ancient scroll paintings.

This area, 'Yun-nan' as it was called, or 'south of the clouds', is spread over 146,700 sq. miles. It is a high table land, intersected by some of the largest rivers of Asia such as the Yangtse, Mekong, Salween, and the eastern branch of the Irrawadi. The intervening mountain ranges reach heights of 22,000 feet crowned by eternal snows.

Exotic fruits like kiwi, mango, banana, and papaya grow in abundance in the hilly regions, interspersed by heavy mahogany, teak, camphor, and sandalwood forests. The tiger shared this land with other species which are now also endangered such as elephants, Malay bears, leopards, rhinoceros, and a variety of rare birds.

The presence of the tiger in Chinese life is also revealed by this piece of 'Feng-Shui' advice: 'When you get halfway up, you will see tigers with their mouths wide open waiting to devour you. Carry some hemp on your back, and when a tiger attempts to bite you, let him bite the hemp, and make your escape.'

Amongst the Ch'uan Miao, diseases and many other disasters were considered to have been caused by demons, and the cure lay in exorcizing these demons, a task for the 'Tuan kung' or exorcist. The Ch'uan Miao believed that people could change into buffaloes, cows, tigers, foxes, monkeys, rats, snakes, fish, frogs, crabs, flowers, vines, and banana trees and then back again into human beings. The transformation of men into tigers or tigers into men was supposed to be common. Men could turn into 'evil tigers', or deceased fathers could change into 'good tigers' to help their sons. A witch called 'bontsong' could bewitch people and change them into tigers.

As Perceval Yelts commented on the centrality of the tiger in Chinese life in 1912,

Just as the dragon is chief of all aquatic creatures, so is the tiger lord of land animals. These two share the position of prime importance in the mysterious pseudo-science called Feng-Shui. The tiger is figured on many of the most ancient bronzes, and its head is still reproduced as an ornament on the sides of bronzes and porcelain vessels, often with a ring in its mouth. It frequently appears in a grotesque form which native archaeologists designate a 'quadruped'. The tiger symbolises military prowess. It is an object of special terror to demons and is therefore painted on walls to scare malignant spirits away from the neighborhood of houses and temples.[14]

Many other early travellers in China had also commented on the awe in which the tiger was held, although they sometimes misinterpreted reverence for fear. Heinemann in 1901 stated,

We passed the temple of the Goddess of Mercy Kwanyin Ko; rounded a fantastic-shaped rock resembling a colossal man, called T'aitze-shih (the 'Rock of the heir apparent'), passed a poor looking temple built on a narrow edge, called Kwan-Shin-Po ('Examine the Heart' declivity), whose priest was most anxious to persuade us to stop and breakfast; then to a larger temple, gaudily decorated and in good repair, with a life-sized tiger (image) in a pen and in a small 'joss-house' of its own on the left of the entrance. Propitiating this dreadful being by gifts of incense and the regulation kowtow, the pilgrims hope to secure themselves and their community from his depredations.

Heinemann did not know that the 'dreadful being' was in fact protector, guardian, and God of all forest people.

The white tiger found in India and then cross-bred in captivity all over the world was an integral part of Chinese ritual and belief and must have been a feature of their forests. This white image was regarded as most sacred as the God of the west and controller of wind and water. Thus the symbol of the tiger was placed on the western sides of some Chinese graves.

The tiger since the earliest times figured prominently in the animistic religion of early Chinese nomads, shepherds, and hunters. The white tiger, Pai Hu, represented the west and the autumn, a season of storms. According to popular belief, this season represented the tiger growling and snarling, and on the rampage for a mate. The star Alpha was to the Chinese the reincarnation of the white tiger and lived like a tiger star in the 'silver stream of heaven' known to us as the Milky Way.

For the tiger, Hu, to integrate into the Milky Way, he had to live for 500 years becoming Pai Hu or white tiger, whose immortality would occur in a thousand years when as king of all quadrupeds, he could inhabit the moon or the silver stream of heaven under the new title of Pai Chon Chang. From here he could protect planet earth.

Bernhard Karlgren refers to the strong possibility of the tiger being a fertility symbol, a strong feminine force. It is a Yin animal, full of dark female force. Karlgren concludes, 'Is it too bold, then, to conclude that this "cowry tiger" is a votive symbol, alluding to breeding force in the family?'[15]

The tiger's influence in early Chinese life took a variety of forms. Overall it was a symbol of power and protection. If the dragon was chief of all aquatic creatures, the tiger was the Lord of all land animals. The black and white markings on a tiger's head were believed to be the character Wang or the sign of a king. In early times Chinese soldiers were known to dress in imitation tiger skins with tails for protection against death. A bronze cheek piece in the shape of a tiger's head was also worn. It hung from the helmet and protected the wearer in battle. Early ceremonial vessels had a tiger's or dragon's head with a serpent's tail curling behind, something also found amongst the Nanai in Siberia. Bronze belt hooks in the form of leaping tigers, and jade amulets in the shape of tigers to protect troops in battle indicate its power and the reverence it had.

In later Chinese art from the thirteenth and fourteenth centuries, the tiger was widely depicted on paper scrolls as a symbol of protection against evil.

The tiger was protector of both the living and the dead. It frightened threatening spirits. Its image protected the entrance to tombs. In the first century its image was painted on gateposts of district magistrates' homes. In the Beijing Museum of History, a ferocious tiger stands guard atop the gateway, and on either side are two door gods. Woodblock prints of the tiger hung up at special times of the year, warded off evil. Silver amulets with tiger forms were hung on newly-born sons in the hope that they would be responsible for continuing the family and caring for elders. Mothers would begin sewing shoes, collars, hats, and bibs in different tiger shapes even before childbirth so as to keep away any evil spirit. Boys still receive tiger hats, collars and shoes at one month and on the hundredth day, to protect them. Many hundreds of years ago ceramic factories produced tiger pillows, the only remedy to ward off nightmares and provide a peaceful sleep. Today mothers still make tiger pillows for the safety of the child. Up to 5 years children on special or festive occasions don tiger motifs. The eyes of the tiger especially on shoes, are meant as a guide, helping the child see his path.

In opera and shadow theatre, tiger images, especially with rebel generals, emphasized power and bravery. Tiger chairs were also used in shadow theatre, the lower portion representing the sharp eyes of the tiger and accentuated eyebrows, to provide extra strength to the image.

Deep in the mountains of Tibet, the tiger was ever present. This is indicated by the ritual importance of the very elaborate 'Tiger rugs' of Tibet. They may have been alternatives to tiger skins, which were never easy to come by. They were used in Tibetan Thangkas and for dances during the Tibetan new year, *yogins* sat on them and they were also a seat for Tantrik practitioners. The skin or rug was supposed to keep away snakes, scorpions, insects, and any other natural obstacles. People in authority sat on them while passing verdicts or awarding punishments, as a source of legitimation. They could be a part of the ritual apparel of a throne. When people moved anywhere, carrying their luggage on saddleback, they were covered by tiger rugs for protection. Some rugs came in pairs depicting the concepts of Yin and Yang. Philip Goldman in *The Tiger Rugs of Tibet* states succinctly:

The relevance of the tiger lies in the ambiguous nature of his relationship with man. It mirrors the opposition between men and beasts, nature and civilisation, the controlled and the uncontrolled power. He is the spirit that mediates between the world of the living, and that of those that passed on to the beyond. In this concept, the tiger is one who can transcend the boundaries between both remains. It is herein that rests his symbolic power.[16]

In the dominant Chinese Taoist religion, the universe reflects two opposing yet complementary forces of energy, Yin and Yang, forces that are often wind and water or the tiger and the dragon. In Taoism everything has a soul, be it animate or inanimate. When good it is controlled by Yang or the green dragon, when evil by Yin or the white tiger. The breath of the tiger creates the wind, the breath of the dragon the clouds and together torrents of rain that regenerate the earth and provide vital food for man. In times of severe drought real tiger bones would be dropped into a 'dragon' well, causing such havoc for the reigning dragon that a vast storm would engulf the land causing endless rain.

The first Taoist pope Chang Tao-Ling was said to have been born in AD 35. His search was to find a dragon-tiger elixir for eternal life. He finally found the answer and was able to attain the power of flying, hearing distant sounds, and leaving his body. It is said 'after going through a thousand days of discipline and receiving instruction from a goddess, who taught him to walk about among the stars, he proceeded to fight the king of the demons, to divide mountain and seas and to command the wind and thunder'. The demons fled and Chang Tao-Ling who is considered the true founder of Taoism gained, after nine years, the power to ascend to Heaven. The tiger was his vehicle and he is always depicted riding a tiger. It is the tiger that helped him fight evil and to find the prescription for immortality.

The tiger was an integral part of Chinese medicine with every inch of its physical body having a vital role in the cure of man, from disease.

Fascinating information exists in the *Chinese Materia Medica*, published in 1931 by the Peking Natural History Bulletin on the tiger and its endless uses. It reveals that in 1682, sixty tigers were killed in one day in the mountains of Liaotung; Chinese forests must have been home to a vast amount of tigers. White tigers were called 'Han' and black tigers 'Yu'. There are descriptions of five-toed tigers with horns, which were regarded as amphibious beasts. The following is a description from its pages:

It is the king of the mountain animals. It is shaped like a cat and is the size of a cow. A yellow coat with black spots. Saw-like teeth and hooked claws. Sharp bristle-like whiskers, the tongue is large and broad and full of spikes. Short necked and squat nosed. At night one eye is phosphorescent and provides light while the other eye is used for observation. It roars like thunder and causes a wind to rise. It enters the rutting season the first week of November, others say it comes when the moon is cloudy and that it only copulates once in a lifetime. Gestation is 7 months. The tiger has powers of divination and can sense direction, mark the ground and find food thereby. Men have learnt their ways. In their diet they follow the lunar calendar. During the first half of the month they eat the head end of an animal, during the latter half of the month they eat the tail end. If after 3 attempts it fails to capture an animal it leaves it alone. Dog meat intoxicates tigers.

The smell of burning ram horn will drive them away. While they can kill men and animals, hedgehogs and rats though small can control them.

Pao P'u Tzu said that after 500 years they turn white. Old stories often tell of tigers changing into men and vice versa.[17]

There are also descriptions of tigers that kill only tigers and leopards. They have white bodies with black spots and tails longer than their bodies! Then there are horses that look like tigers—white bodies, black tails, a single horn, and serrated teeth that allow them to eat tigers.

The medicinal qualities of each body part of the tiger are supposed to be unparalleled. The following is a list of the parts, their preparations, and their uses taken from the *Chinese Materia Medica*:

BONE
The bones should be broken open and the marrow removed. Butter or urine or vinegar is applied, according to the type of prescription, and they are browned over a charcoal fire.

Acrid, slightly warming, non-poisonous.

For removing all kinds of evil influences and calming fright. For curing bad ulcers, and rat bite sores. For rheumatic pain in the joints and muscles, and muscle cramps. For abdominal pain, typhoid fever, malaria, and hydrophobia. Placed on the roof it can keep devils away and so cure nightmares. A bath in tiger bone broth is good for rheumatic swellings of the bones and joints. The shinbones are excellent for treating painful swollen feet. It is applied with vinegar to the knees. Newborn children should be bathed in it to prevent infection, convulsions, devil possession, scabies, and boils; they will then grow up without any sickness. It strengthens the bones, cures chronic dysentery, prolepses of the anus, and is taken to dislodge bones, which have become stuck in the gullet. The powdered bone is applied to burns and to eruptions under the toe nail.

THE MAJESTIC BONE OF A TIGER
A curved bone like a character, one inch long, which grows on each side of the chest by the ribs. Worn by officials to give them poise. Non-official people hate them.

TIGER FLESH
Acid, bland, non-poisoning. Said to be bad for the teeth, it should not be eaten in the first lunar month. The taste is not very good; it is earthy though all right salted.

For nausea, improves the vitality, and stops excessive salivation. For malaria. A talisman against thirty-six kinds of demons. A tonic to the stomach and spleen. For eye and rectal diseases—India.

TIGER FAT
For all kinds of vomiting. For dog-bite wounds. Applied in the rectum for bleeding haemorrhoids. Melted and applied to scab and bald-headed condition in children.

TIGER BLOOD
It builds up the constitution and strengthens will-power.

STOMACH OF THE TIGER
To cure vomiting and to quieten the stomach.

TESTES OF THE TIGER
For scrofula.

BILE OF THE TIGER

For convulsions in children. For 'Kan' dysentery in children with restlessness and nervousness.

EYEBALL OF THE TIGER

Eyeballs are not used from animals that have died of sickness. The ball is macerated overnight in fresh sheep's blood, then separated and dried over a low flame and powdered.

For epilepsy, malaria, fevers in children, and convulsions. For quietening nervous children. It clarifies the vision and removes membranes over the eye. It stops crying.

THE SHADE OF A TIGER

A mythological thing said to be found in the ground, an amber-like stone, which falls from the glance of a dying tiger when it is shot. Recommended for convulsions in children. Ordinary amber Hu P'o is a term derived from this, the idea being that the soul of the animal turns into a mineral.

THE NOSE OF THE TIGER

For epilepsy and for convulsions in children. Hung on the roof it will induce the birth of boys.

TIGER TEETH

Applied to sores on the penis and running sores. Taken for hydrophobia and phthisis.

TIGER CLAWS

With the bones and hair of the paw of the male animal tied on a baby's arm as a talisman.

TIGER SKIN

For malaria and to keep away evil influences. Ashed and taken for infectious fevers. It is not good to sleep on, it induces fear, and the hair is very poisonous to open wounds.

TIGER'S WHISKERS

Given for toothache.

TIGER'S FAECES

Mixed with horse's urine and ashed, the dust is applied to whitlows. It is also used for bad boils and piles. It is taken to remove bones stuck in the gullet.

BONES IN TIGER'S FAECES
Sliced and ashed.
For burns and tetanus and to treat alcoholism.[18]

Moreover the image of the tiger was said to act like a charm against spectral influences. A likeness of the animal in any form was a protection against disease. A tiger's claw averted evil, small bones of the feet were potent charms and prevented convulsions in children, spectral fevers were cured by touching the skin, and as a door charm it was the destroyer and expeller of spectres. The tiger attacked evil, and even fevers that were incurable were said to be cured by reading verses on tigers! The flesh of the tiger was supposed to prevent stomach and spleen disorders. Pills from the eyeballs were supposed to cure convulsions. The whiskers and claws provided great strength and courage, the skin burnt and roasted was a cure for all ills especially when mixed with water; other parts were prized for their aphrodisiacal properties, tiger grease diluted with oil cured stomach ailments, bones from the end of the tail and floating ribs were supposed to destroy evil and bring good luck and fortune.

Further,

When the tigress produces young, each is born with a snake wound round its neck. These snakes may bite people, but the bite will never prove fatal.

The gallstone of the tiger if applied to the eyes will strengthen them. It will also stop the eyes from persistent watering. From the gallstone may also be brewed a most virulent poison, which will cause instant death. If the severed head of the tiger becomes rotten, then whoever smells it will die.

If the hair of a tiger is burnt it will drive out all the centipedes from that place. If one tahil [one and one-third ounce] of tiger flesh is consumed, then whoever consumes it will be impervious to snake bite. If the skin is sat upon while naked then the patient will be cured of certain types of sickness.

The brain mixed with aged oil when rubbed on the body will cure laziness or pimples.

The tail, dried and ground to powder, if mixed with soap will produce an ointment which, when used while bathing, will cure skin diseases.

The gallstone mixed with honey, will cure abscesses of the hand and feet.

If the fat is dried and a mixture made from it with flour and garlic, then no feline animal will attack those who rub it on their body. Fat from a tiger's face is mixed with the essence of roses. If this is rubbed on the face then the user of it will be honoured by all who meet him including princes.[19]

The Chinese believed that a vital fluid existed in the tiger's bones which, when cooked and mixed with medicaments, protected against evil dreams and strange fevers. There was also a medicine made from the liver that was considered to have the highest of healing qualities.

Even people who were tormented by ghosts were advised to drink soup made from the skin of a tiger for cure! This provided a vital cure for any mental illness also.

Above all, the tiger was supposed to have incredible sexual prowess. Able to copulate several times an hour and even over a hundred times in a few days, his penis was much in demand as a most powerful aphrodisiac.

How was the tiger then able to survive so long in China when every body part was widely sought after for its supposed medicinal value? The answer lies in that the lives of man and tiger were intimately linked, and before the advent of the gun, although tigers were killed on ceremonial occassions, there was no mass or wanton destruction. China's forests were thus full of tigers.

In the middle of the nineteenth century tigers were very common in southern China, and this was the home of one of the four Chinese sub-species, the South China tiger, which was a little smaller than its Indian counterpart. At this time a few tigers were found in Hupeh, in the rocky gorges of Changyang and Patung. Very few were found in western Szechwan but they were more common in the Chienchang valley and southward to Yunan. The tiger freely roamed the mountains of Yenpayi, west of Wanhsien and in Dijinshan. They were found even in Amoy and one was reported to have swum to Amoy city on an island where it was eventually killed. They were also found in southern Kwangtung, the mountain regions of Tanhashan, and in Fukien. Tracks were reported in Anhwei, Chekiang, and the Kekwan mountains, and in western Shansi. A 'black' tiger was reported killed near Hangchow in the Eastern Tombs forest in 1912. Canton, Foochow, and Nanking all abounded with tigers.

This detailed description of the tiger comes from Major H.R. Davies late last century:

Soon after starting the next morning we heard the roaring of a tiger in the hills to the west across the river. Though evidently he was not far off we could not make him out for some time, but finally he came out and lay down on a big rock to sun himself. He was about 600 yards off on a steep hillside and as there was no means of crossing the river which lay between him and us, it was impossible to get nearer to have a shot. The tiger did not seem the least disturbed by our watching him, nor by the presence of several people who were going along a path on his side of the river about 500 yards below him. I took out my field glasses and watched him for about five minutes. Eventually he got up and walked away into the jungle. This is the first tiger I have seen or heard of in Western China, though I have occasionally come across panther tracks. It is not often in any country that one would get such a good look at a tiger and such an opportunity of observing his ways.[20]

But life in China was changing and new weapons, religions, beliefs, the booming fur trade, and receding forests, were about to take their toll on the lives of the forest people and their guardian and protector, the tiger. A traditional culture was about to fade away.

R.C. Andrews talks of Fukien early this century:

The larger part of Fukien, like many other provinces in China, has been denuded of forests, and the groves of pines which remain have all been planted. This deforestation consequently has driven out the game, and except for

tigers, leopards, wolves, wild pigs, serows and gorals none of the large species is left.[21]

Discussing the fur trade, he states, 'Pandas were supposed to be exceedingly rare and we could hardly believe it possible when we saw dozens of coats made of their skins hanging in the shops.'

He goes on to say that every year a few tiger skins find their way to Hsiakuan from the southern part of the province along the Tonking border, but the good ones are quickly sold at prices varying from 25–50 dollars (Mexican).

It was in the Fukien province that R.C. Andrews encountered H.R. Caldwell who did a painstaking and detailed study of the South China tiger in Fukien or for that matter anywhere in China. R.C. Andrews states of Caldwell,

He almost invariably went on foot from place to place and carried with him a butterfly net and a rifle, so that to so keen a naturalist each day's walk was full of interest.

During his many experiences with tigers Mr Caldwell has learned much about their habits and peculiarities.[22]

But what is remarkable is that in China where white and black as well as ordinary tigers were recorded, Caldwell found the only case of a 'blue tiger'. He states:

The markings of the animal were marvellously beautiful. The ground colour seemed to be a deep shade of Maltese, changing into almost deep blue on the under parts. The stripes were well defined, and so far as I was able to make out, similar to those on a tiger of the regular type.[23]

Caldwell tried desperately to hunt this tiger but was unsuccessful. Andrews accompanied him and though very close to it never saw it, but he believed it to be blue and states, 'I believed then, and my opinion has since been strengthened, that it is a partially Melanistic phase of the ordinary yellow tiger.'[24] The local people of this area referred to the tiger as 'bluebeard' or 'black devil' and Caldwell found evidence of the 'black devil', many years later after this first sighting.

Caldwell spent twenty-four years in China as a Christian missionary in an attempt to advance the knowledge of Christianity in Asia. Focusing his efforts in Fukien, a region abounding in tigers, where man and tiger mutually respected each other, and where the tiger was an energy that was worshipped, Caldwell started his missionary activity, described in a chapter called 'A Rifle as a Calling Card', by boasting of the virtues of his very fancy gun, a weapon that had never been seen in the area. A man who dripped with arrogance about the American way of life and religion, Caldwell's methods of conversion were crude attempts at establishing the inferiority of Chinese belief and superiority of the Western.

Described in his book *Blue Tiger* are his methods. In an area where forest communities never slaughtered tigers, for their supernatural energies were to be propitiated, Caldwell knocked off tigers with his gun. He states, 'Before we ended our conversation Elder Ding remarked: "Teacher, I am afraid those people would not have heard of Christ until this day had you not killed that tiger." Again a gun had been used to preach the first sermon in a community of villages.'

There is little doubt that Christianity and imperialism had a major hand in changing a way of life that had an intimate dependence on nature. But communism too played a part. In fact, every political regime in the twentieth century has operated with a complete disregard for the fine balance between man and nature. Under the communists, in fact, the tiger was declared a pest.

According to Dr Lu Houji of the East China Normal University,

From the early 1950s hunters were encouraged to kill tigers and a bounty was even paid for each one. In 1977 the government belatedly woke up to the fact that the tiger population had decreased alarmingly. In an effort to stop the decline a law was passed forbidding the hunting of all tiger sub-species. Unfortunately this law could not be strictly enforced and hunting continued. With the scarcity of tigers a black market ensued. Now poaching is the overriding cause of the decline of the tiger.[25]

Laws and legislations in themselves are ineffective when the way of life that linked the tiger to man has vanished.

There are hardly 30–50 South China tigers left today and it was only in 1981 that one of its last refuges in Guangdong Province was declared a protected area and became the Chebaling reserve. The tiger will probably soon become extinct in China with little left to show for its long sojourn there, apart from some sterile hangovers from the past.

Into the New Territories and Hong Kong

The tiger's remarkable swimming prowess also made it an occasional visitor to Hong Kong, crossing from mainland China at points where the distance between the two is only 1 km. A description of tigers in Hong Kong comes from G.A.C. Herklots, published in 1951 by the *South China Morning Post*:

Nearly every winter one or more tigers visit the New Territories; often the visitor is a tigress with or without cubs. The visit rarely lasts more than two or three days. A tiger thinks nothing of a 40-mile walk and in a couple of nights could walk from the wild country behind Bias Bay to Tai Mo Shao or the Kowloon hills. Because their visits are usually of such short duration and because most people exaggerate, little credence is given to tiger rumours. Most that I have investigated have been founded on fact.

In 1915 a tiger was shot by Mr Burlingham A.S.P. in the New Territories but only after it had killed Sergeant Groucher and, I believe, two Indian constables. I once had a copy of the account of the hunt for this animal: if my memory is correct I believe it was reported to have visited both Hong

Kong Island and Lan Tau island in its wanderings. Since then, notably in 1925, there have been several reports of a tiger or tigress with cubs having been seen in the New Territories. A few more recent accounts are given below.

On the afternoon of 29th December, 1929, a Chinese village woman was driving a cow to the village of Fung Yuen at the eastern side of Tolo Harbour opposite Tai Po. Near a ravine, bordered by thick scrub, about a mile from the village, a tiger sprang out from the thicket onto the back of the cow biting and mauling the animal severely. The cow struggled on for 100 yards, lay down and died. Sergeant Tuckett visited the spot and examined the cow, which showed unmistakable signs of having been mauled by a tiger. On the same afternoon a tiger was reported at Cha Hang about two miles away.

On 4th January, 1931, it was reported that a tigress with two cubs had been seen at Pan Chung near Tai Po Market.

On 2nd November, 1934, a tiger was reported to have visited the village of Lo Wai, Tsun Wan, on the previous night and to have carried off a pig weighing approximately 60 catties (80 lbs). The next day one fore foot only of the victim was discovered under a bush. A fortnight later the same Chinese reported that the tiger had appeared again and had killed three pigs of about 20 catties weight each. The officer in charge of Tsun Wan police station saw two of the carcasses and noted the marks of the killer's fangs. Towards the end of the month a large pig disappeared from the village of Tsung Lung. Next day a village dog was seen carrying the snout of the missing pig. On 30th December three men were shooting francolins on the hills behind the village of Tai Wo in the direction of Tang Um. It began to rain. A distant roar was heard which one of the Chinese of the party said was a tiger. Within a minute another roar was heard and a Ha Ka woodcutter then drew the attention of the three to a tiger 400 or 500 yards away. It walked unconcernedly into the heavily wooded hillside only about 3 miles from Lo Wai, Tsun Wan.

The next day the Chinese, who had originally brought the first news of the animal, said that it had again been seen on 29th December and had chased a deer. The deer had been so frightened that it ran through the village and got stuck in a marshy pig-weed pond 30 yards from the main road and was caught by a Chinese. The tiger did not run through the village but roamed about in some vegetable gardens just outside. Here its pugmarks measured 7 1/2 inches across both ways, excluding 1/8 inch on each side to allow for crumbling of the earth. This tiger probably weighed about 200 lbs.

This animal was seen again twice. An old woman grass-cutter was returning home from Tsun Wan when the tiger walked up to her and started to circle round her. She was terrified but when it came too close she summoned up courage to give it a few blows with her pole (for carrying the grass) and managed to scare it away. When interviewed later the woman was still in hysterics. On 28th January 1935, it again visited Lo Wai, Tsun Wan, but failed to secure any food. It was not seen again. This tiger had thus been about in the Tai Mo Shan district for nearly three months, an unusually long stay. It probably moved about a good bit for one was heard grunting on Ng Tung Shan just across the border by a friend of mine and might well have been the same animal. It had killed a bullock and was grunting over its kill but my friend was not told this till he had descended the mountain.

One day I received a telephone message from a police friend that two tigers had been seen near Kowloon reservoir—only a mile or two from the city. I sent two Chinese to investigate and gave them a bag of plaster-of-Paris and asked them to return with casts of the pugmarks. They returned with three or four excellent casts but even then many doubted the tale.

During our internment at Stanley a remarkable story filtered into the camp that there was a tiger at large on Hong Kong Island. Later it was reported to be on Stanley peninsula; our Formosan guards got very excited and it was risky walking about in the evening for an excited guard might fire at a prisoner mistaking him for a tiger. Soon pugmarks were seen in the camp. I examined some myself but was by no means convinced. Then the story was spread that the tiger had been shot and finally there came into camp a Chinese or Japanese paper containing a photograph of the dead tiger. This photograph I saw. People said that it was a menagerie animal that had got loose, a likely story! It is strange how loath people are to believe that tigers do visit the Colony and occasionally swim the harbour and visit the Island.[26]

The skin of this tiger is still to be found in the Tin Han temple in Stanley village.

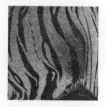

Into Indo-China

From southern China the tiger passed into Indo-China, Vietnam, Laos and Cambodia, and some probably entered Burma and India.

Vietnam stretches over 1000 miles from the misty mountains on the Chinese border to the flat Mekong delta, with diverse bays like Ha Long where strangely shaped lime rock mountains jut out of the emerald sea, while fishing junks ply in and out of the quiet waters. The mountainous regions offer majestic views of jungle-covered mountains and primeval tropical forests. On the delta the sun is fierce, but cool shade is provided by banana and coconut trees.

This area was under French control by 1883 and the first descriptions of these jungles came from French administrators turned hunters. William Baze in *Tiger Tiger* describes the area as it was early last century:

In the high plateau of the Moi hinterland lying in the centre of Indo-China where Vietnam, Cambodia and Laos all meet, the forest clearings are always covered with pines and other conifers. In South Vietnam, in the neighborhood of Phanrang, the general desolation of the scenery is enhanced by the fantastic bare silhouettes of stunted trees standing up gaunt in the grassy plain. This kind of country crops up again at Son Phan, an area near the border of South Annam which is very rich in game of all kinds, especially the big grey ox and the little red one. In Cambodia these clearings are often visited by cow-prey and in Laos by a smaller species of gaur, deer, goats, muntjacs, wild boar and agoutis usually to be found in the forest clearing; so also is the tiger, who comes here to escape from the wood-leech, elsewhere so abundant.

Whole forests of dwarf bamboo grow in these parts, also a shrub peculiar to the 'red earth' lands of east Cochin China. Stretches of trench alternate with thick clumps and woods of enormous trees growing from the depth of the ravines.

Another feature of the landscape in Indo-China is the great Savannah, where the reeds grow as high as an elephant and are the principal crop. Every year in January and February the Savannah is swept by great fires from which it takes a month to recover.

One part of the country I knew very well was Co Hen, a remote district, very rich in tigers, lying between the last of the Lagna Savannahs and the first outcrops of the Annamese mountains, where the tigers were well settled in. It was a delightful spot. The forests in the dry season and the plains in the rainy reason were full of roots, grasses, fruits and young shoots of all kinds.[27]

Here the tiger interfaced with forest dwellers called Mnong or Moi. The Mnong shared a deep complementarity with nature, ensuring the regeneration of what they took from it. This changed with the arrival of the Europeans. This is revealed in an incident that occurred late last century where a geodetical survey required the cutting down of a tree to operate certain instruments. The chief of the coolies, a Mnong, approached the tree and addressed it,

Spirit who last made thy home in this tree, we worship thee and are come to claim thy mercy. The white mandarin, our relentless master, whose commands we cannot but obey, has bidden us to cut down thy habitation, a task that fills us with sadness and which we only carry out with regret. I adjure thee to depart at once from the place and seek a new dwelling place elsewhere, and I pray thee to forget the wrong we do thee, for we are not our own masters.[28]

This communication to the spirit of the tree was concluded by another to the king of the forest, the tiger, who has jurisdiction over each tree in the area. The Mnong believe that the tiger is first among animals and has intense supernatural powers. They refer to him with respect and fear as 'king of the mountain', 'his eminence', 'my lord', 'the gentleman', 'the master', 'lofty one', and never by the name 'tiger'.

Once while trapping deer, a tiger was caught in a Mnong trap. Terrified that it might die, they decided to set it free by lowering a cage without a floor into the pit and raising it, after passing ropes under the tiger. From perches on trees, the tiger was pulled up and freed, and a string of apologies offered for having delayed it so long in a pit.

On another occasion a tiger that had killed someone was completely forgiven by the victim's uncle who said, 'My brother should know, that the spirits of my relations who never received burial, nor the rites that were their due have long demanded another companion.' It was genuinely believed that the tiger only killed men who were evil, or who had sinned.

Sometimes at the spot where a tiger has killed a man, a ceremony is conducted where the image of the tiger with three figures on its back is drawn on a piece of paper. The paper is then solemnly burnt and the ashes scattered over the tomb amidst much prayer and reverence. Memorial stones for the tiger are also created at such spots, with the image of the tiger painted on stone. The altar has a niche where joss sticks burn so as to please the spirit of the tiger and the forest and anyone who passes would pray and offer something.

Even if a village is plagued by a marauding tiger, the Mnong would rather abandon it for a new one than kill the tiger. They also place a box with an image of the tiger carved on one side. Anyone who passes the spot will leave a stone or twig in honour of the tiger spirit. This spirit is invoked at critical times, and images of the tiger are found on the walls of temples, pagodas, houses, stone screens, and even children's cradles. The tiger is the Mnong guardian.

The Mnong believe that there is fearsome power in the whiskers of the tiger, which can be the source of a fatal poison. The whiskers are enclosed in hollow bamboo sticks. After many 'watches' a snake will emerge from the bamboo, and once a year the medicine man will feed the snake grains of maize and the snake will provide the drops of poison. The poison must be used by a certain time against whosoever the spirits choose.

The Mnong also believe that a tiger that is clumsy enough to damage the ear of its victim in an attack will abandon it immediately and never return to eat it. They believe that when a tiger kills a man, it looses a bit of its ear. The number of chunks missing from the tiger's ear reveal the number of its victims. The Mnong are convinced that the tiger can hear everything about himself even from 'a thousand leagues away' and exacts revenge for any insults. According to the Mnong, the tiger can transform himself into a human being and speak.

The Mnong invoke the spirit of grain before every harvest through a complicated process of ritual and ceremony in which the sacrifice of a pig or chicken completes the offering to the spirit. This worship of grain is interlinked to tiger worship to pray for a rich harvest.

Sickness, mental or physical, is ascribed to possession by an evil spirit and a shaman is called in to exorcize the spirit. In the words of an early traveller,

Then to the accompaniment of a series of peculiar writhing movements she chants a litany, which gets quicker and quicker as the candles get smaller. Her contortions also become more rapid and violent and in the end she is seized with a fit of hysterics, which signifies the frantic struggle of the 'PI' before they yield to the power of the incantation. All at once her movement ceases and she commences to indicate the hour in which the cure will take place.[29]

For the purpose of exorcism, many different spirits can be invoked, especially the spirit of the tiger.

Mnong medicine is as dependent on a tiger's body as Chinese but unlike the Chinese, before the advent of the gun the Mnong only killed a tiger for ceremonial purposes. Teeth and claws provide charms to ward off evil as do the small bones of the shoulder. Teeth are also filed to cure dog bites. The powder is diluted in water and produces a foolproof remedy. When a man-eater was killed [mainly by European hunters] a cigarette holder was made from the canine so as to reveal the victim's image when it got blackened by the smoke.

The nerves are carefully cleaned and mixed with alcohol. The beverage is an elixir for long life and a potent aphrodisiac. Again some inherent connection is suggested between fertility and immortality.

The Mnong also shatter the skull and jaw of a dead tiger and bury the pieces separately so that the soul of 'the lord' does not appear headless to frighten their communities.

The Mnong have a complete understanding of nature and rely on other animals and birds to give an unfailing indication of a tiger's presence. Thus the Moi saying, 'The owl's cry indicates the devil's presence and that of the crow the tiger's presence.'

Describing the 'closeness' of the Moi to nature and the tiger, William Baze states,

One of my Moi trackers could give a perfect imitation of a young deer in distress, using a tiny 'bird call' made from a palm leaf. By cunning modulations he could even make it sound as if the little animal was running around looking for its mother. Eight times out of ten, especially round about twilight, a tiger would come to investigate.[30]

Baze hunted many tigers with the Mnong and reflected on their uncanny reverence for this animal.

Despite the depredations of these thieving old tigers, these villagers never take any sensible steps to get rid of them.

The local magicians may see these man-eaters as unfortunate creatures haunted by departed spirits thirsting for vengeance, and if that is their view, these tigers must not be hunted: they must instead be treated with every respect and consideration. The magician has been known to carry this farce to the point where the villagers have been exhorted to leave their homes altogether so as to avoid upsetting the spirits. The result has been a mass migration.

Elsewhere he states,

The man-eater had a strange preference for the opposite sex, since in five weeks he had taken two women before this one. The magician spoke of metempsychosis. According to him this tiger was inhabited by the soul of a deceived husband. That was enough for the Moi. A wave of marital fidelity immediately swept through the village and all the married folk enjoyed, thanks to the tiger, a second honeymoon! . . .

He used to burn joss sticks before the little altars erected by passers-by in honour of the tiger. These altars marked dangerous tracks from which unfortunate pilgrims had never returned. . . .

Cai Tan would spontaneously make an offering to the spirits every time he killed a tiger which he thought might have eaten human flesh, firm in the belief that the homeless souls of the departed which had inhabited the tiger were now set free and must be appeased. . . .

But somewhere the Moi believed that the presence of the tiger was virtuous in spirit or reality. They knew that when their crops were being destroyed by other animals it was always the tiger that stepped in to provide justice. The tiger often helped them to preserve a piece of rice or maize in some isolated square of mountainous region. They revered it as a gentleman.[31]

The Mnong live in houses made of bamboo and rattan with walls and roofs of grass. These houses are placed on stilts as protection from tigers and snakes. It is said that the Mnongs are so nimble that they are able to use their toes almost like fingers to pick up anything from the ground without stooping. The Mnong are relieved if they see a tiger yawn, for it signifies, especially at noon, that he relieves his memory and spits out anything that might have been said against him. It is like a frequent cleansing of the slate and the Mnong are grateful for this.

In the elaborate ritual and ceremony that accompany childbirth, the tiger has a prescriptive role. If a dog steps over a newborn, people shout and chase the dog away. They say, 'May the tiger devour you,' for a strict rule has been violated and the dog will be killed that day. Other taboos of childbirth, if not observed, it is believed, would call on the wrath of the tiger as punishment.

In fact, in general, the tiger has a prescriptive role, with societal codes often being enforced through fear of a tiger's attack being invoked on violators.

With the advent of the hunter and his modern gun, the relationship between tiger and tribe must have been severely scarred. Some descriptions by hunters early in the twentieth century vividly bring to life Indo-China's tiger-infested jungles.

Mary Hastings Bradley in *Trailing the Tiger* describes the tiger trail from India to Burma to Java and Sumatra and finally to Vietnam, where she saw and shot a tiger.

Our camp on the Lang Bian plateau was a most lovely spot. We were on a highland among tall pine trees that were spaced as if planted in a park, so that one could see for long distances except when bushes intervened. It was, of course, a perfectly natural growth but so different from the density of our pine forests at home that it was a constant marvel.

These trees were about sixty years old, and some distance to the north another forest began, rather sharply differentiated, with trees a hundred years old, and further north, were other forests yet older as if the armies of great pines, marching south from China, were flinging out battalions of young trees ahead of them.

The highlands were cut sharply by steeply sloped ravines, jungles choked at the bottom, where rivers and streams wandered through the thickets. Here in the jungles the tigers lurked, except in the rainy season, when they roamed everywhere in the tall grass. . . .

They were very wonderful, those walks through the jungle at night. I think we were quite mad in what we did, though we liked to think then that we were being cautious, moving carefully and keeping a wary outlook.

The lights on our heads made the rest of the world utterly dark, though the soft stars were pouring down a still radiance. We moved through a black velvet scene, the headlights picking one object at a time out of the gloom, now the round bole of a pine tree, now a feathery shrub, now a plumed spear of waving grass . . . very often we heard the startled snort of some astonished beast. Once a stag crashed out of the depths of a dewy thicket where it had been asleep.

We stopped softly, the night wind blowing in our faces, attended only by that ghostly ray of light in the vast darkness. . . . We had an extraordinary sense of solitude.

It seemed strange to us that there were people anywhere who elected to stay in their beds, or yawn at plays, or doze at operas. They should come out at night, on foot, into tiger land, step by step into the mysterious dark, with a thread of light throwing its will-o'-the-wisp ray into the shadows . . . listening to the bark of the deer and the leopards cry . . . hearing soft rustles that make them stiffen in their tracks and their blood pound so that it seemed the tigers thud . . . the taste of life was never so keen on my lips as in those times.[32]

She describes her first tiger:

There was a feeling in the air that the day was done. And then, as I looked out, realising every moment slipping by as something palpable, bearing forever away the chances it might have held—I saw something.

Out of the wall of distant shadows came a gleam of gold and black— vivid as lighting against the green—and the tiger walked out of the jungle.

Never in my life had I seen such a picture. Elephants by moonlight, lions at dawn, gorillas at blazing noon I had seen, but nothing was ever so beautiful and so glorious to me as that tiger walking out of his jungle. He was everything that was wild and savage, lordly and sinister.

He seemed to materialize like something in a dream and for a moment I could imagine I was dreaming. He stood, projected vividly against the forest, and he looked enormous. The great striped roundness of him was like a barrel. Then he moved, and seemed to flow along the ground, nearer and nearer.[33]

Bradley's description seems to ascribe a spiritual quality to a tiger sighting, something that reduced the watcher to a dream-like state.

Baze provides an interesting example of communal living among tigers.

A typical example of this communal living was to be found at the caves of Pou Na Khlong in the heart of the jungle. When the seasonal fires were sweeping the plains, the primeval forest of Tra Hon also remained a green oasis in a desert of arid desolation. Similarly, when the annual floods drowned the valley of the Lagna River, the little island of Bau Dien, refuge of all the terrified animals of the whole region, were spared even in the worst of times.

Before us lay a great jumble of rocks, surmounted by an immense bare plateau. An astonishing labyrinth, born of one of nature's wildest dreams, was split into innumerable cracks and heaped into fantastic blocks of incredible shapes and sizes. Here and there the rocks were banded together with clay, but for the most part it was a colossal jumble of loose boulders and great yawning chasms. In several places the rock face was hallowed into shallow caves, reached by steep rocky little tracks, which could possibly be used by a tiger; one of them bigger than the rest, looked as though it might be the main entrance to the caves. The earth all round was clear of all grass and had no doubt been worn smooth by the tigers' feet. Twenty or thirty feet higher was a range of smaller caves inaccessible to the tigers; these were the home of a whole tribe of monkeys. Tough plants and tree creepers gave access from the upper caves to the tops of the trees and provided them with a marvellous playground.

They were delightful little fellows, black and white collars, and they seemed quite undisturbed by our presence. Those nearest to us would hang on to the thick creepers and make comic faces at us while they shook them as if they were trying to shake apples down from the trees, and others performed incredible balancing feats for our delight.[34]

Baze found and killed six tigers that lived in these labyrinthine caves with their extraordinary caverns and annexes. The corners were full of bones of animals that the tigers must have fed on. There were dark narrow passages opening out into the 'rooms'.

Actually there was only one complete family living here—the tigress, her cubs, and the big tiger my friend shot. Another tiger—the one I accounted for—lived by himself in a separate apartment, and the last tigress lived in another cul-de-sac with the baby whose body we found. The maize of caverns and passages provided a safe retreat, sheltered from bad weather, and they would sally forth, separately at night to scour the countryside, keeping as far as possible out of one another's way.

Reflecting on his experience of Indo-China and its tiger, Baze says:

So I ask you which is the more bloodthirsty, tiger or man? Anyway, I was able now and then to lift a corner of the curtain behind which so many dramas were being played on that magnificent stage, the jungles of Indo-China. In the heart of the vast and virgin forest the great spectacle was revealed as the years rolled by, always magnificent and always changing. So remote seemed all the deceptive activity, all the squalid restlessness of civilisation, that life there with my Moi friends seemed to be out of this world. They were primitive and simple minded, and in their company I spent the happiest hours of my life, reading in the great open book of nature, seeking always to probe its mysteries and discover its secrets. Now I am buried deep—against my will—in the noisy whirl of a great city, and I find myself longing once more for that clean and healthy freedom of body and soul which I knew in the luxuriant forests or on the limitless savannahs where the giant crickets used to sing their discordant songs.

Is it nostalgia for the measureless tropical horizons that eats at my heart during these cold nights in Paris? Or has some mysterious forest fever turned the blood in my veins to ice?

I only know that I am always seeing, as if I were there in the flesh, the people and things I loved—my gay half-naked Moi, the warm, silent night, black as velvet, yet starred by the beam of my night-hunter's torch and by whole constellations of glowing eyes; great bellowing herds of elephants with waving trunks and fearsome tusks.[35]

Some hunters were not so lucky. They found it exceedingly difficult to organize hunts or to find beaters to flush the forest for the attempt alone was regarded as a sign of disrespect to the tiger, and the whole village could suffer later on. The disaster of losing a member of the village in such a hunt would be major, for if the bones were not found and a burial ceremony not organized, the agonized spirit would turn into an evil one to seek revenge for generations. Hunters would suddenly find small altars and temples deep in the forest where images of the tiger would remind them of the deep feelings of reverence that the Mnong had towards this animal.

Once after killing a tigress who was harmless and unafraid of human beings, Baze states, 'The magicians, of course were not to be put off with any such simple explanation. They organised an elaborate ceremony to appease the spirit of the dead tigress and everybody did honour to the occasion, bending the elbow energetically and loudly proclaiming the dawn of a new era.'

The French did their damage in Indo-China, be it on people, their culture, the forest, or the tiger, the hunter took his toll in the areas; but this was nothing compared to what was to come.

The Indo-Chinese region has been ravaged by violence, uprising, and war and in the last decades, hundreds of thousands have lost their lives, huge forest tracts have been fired by napalm, and the earth has been shaken by frequent and repeated barrages of bullets and bombs. After the return of some peace and until only recently, they say that the tiger still walks in pockets of this area. There could still be 200–300 tigers roaming the jungles of Indo-China, invisible to all except the Mnongs who must have lived through hell in the years of war. Of late, they have been held responsible for killing the few remaining tigers in this area. However, the responsibility for destroying the tigers' traditional rhythm of life lies elsewhere, and at that door must also be laid the responsibility of endangering the Indo-Chinese tiger.

Into Thailand

The tiger then squeezed into Thailand. The 1500 km. of land from north to south is one of varying climate, the north a monsoon belt with long dry periods and the south with frequent rainfall and tropical

flavour, and countless beaches, coasts and bays. The Thais probably came from southern China but according to early records, the first inhabitants were the Monsa people from the subcontinent who settled in the early centuries of the Christian era on the lower reaches of the Chao Phya River.

An early traveller in the nineteenth century writes of the Thai country,

In this part of the country the Siamese declare they cannot cultivate bananas on account of the elephants, which at certain times come down from the mountains and devour the leaves of which they are very fond. The royal and other tigers abound here; every night they prowl about in the vicinity of the houses and in the mornings we can see the print of their large claws in the sand and in the clay near streams. By day they retire to the mountains, where they lurk in close and inaccessible thickets. Now and then you may get near enough to one to have a shot at him, but generally, unless suffering from hunger, they fly at the approach of man.[36]

Describing his feelings in the forest at the border of Thailand and Laos he writes,

I am at the gates of the internal regions, for so the Laotians and Siamese designate this forest, and I have no spell to terrify the demons which inhabit it, neither tiger's teeth or stunted stag-horn; nothing but my faith in and love for God. If I must die here, where so many other wanderers have left their bones, I shall be ready when my hour comes.

The profound stillness of this forest, and its luxuriant tropical vegetation, are indescribable, and at this midnight hour impress me deeply. The sky is serene, the air fresh, and the moon's rays only penetrate here and there, through the foliage, in patches, which appear on the ground like pieces of white paper dispersed by the wind. Nothing breaks the silence but a few dead leaves rustling to the earth, the murmur of a brook which flows.[37]

In these border areas of Laos, Thailand, and Cambodia, the forest people, especially in Cambodia, believed that if they ate certain types of wild rice that grow in thick swamps they could change into tigers, and women, by rubbing a magical ointment on their body and rushing into the forests could change into tigresses in seven days. People like the 'Khon Lamoh' in Thailand also believed that men could change into tigers by using magical formulae but these beliefs seemed to peak as the tiger moved further south.

But Thailand changed drastically during the twentieth century with increasing population, widespread and unregulated intensive cultivation and forest husbandry, taking their toll on nature and the tiger. A traditional ecological pattern was dying, its links with nature were fading, and a new way of life emerging.

One of the last refuges of the tiger in Thailand is the Khao Yai National Park, an area encompassing 2168 sq. km. It is mountainous country, with peaks as high as 1350 m. The area receives two monsoon rains and the average rainfall is 3000 mm. It is one of the last intact tropical forest tracts of mainland Asia and most of the Park is covered by dry and semi-evergreen rainforests with the mountains clothed in hill evergreen forests.

In 1977 the population of tigers in Thailand was estimated at 500–600. It seems to be concentrated in the Tenassarin range towards the Thai–Burmese border. Here the tiger feeds most commonly on barking deer but the current population of the tiger could have gone down to 250 or even less.

Into Malaysia

From Thailand the tiger passed into Malaysia where it thrived, deeply influencing people and their rituals. The Europeans have left several accounts of the hypnotic effect of the tiger encountered in Malaysia's forests, of beats and hunts, and of the tiger's importance in Malay custom and life, attesting to the abundance of the tiger in Malaysia.

Malaysia was probably one of the earliest sites inhabited by man as is attested by archaeological discoveries at the Niah limestone caves in Sarawak's 4th Division, where ancient relics dating back 50,000 years have been found. The aboriginal mountain people of peninsular Malaysia are evidence of Malaysia's occupation before the arrival of the Malays.

Said Colonel Locke:

To this day I can close my eyes and see the tiger standing there as though we had confronted each other but a moment ago. The torch did not light up the animal distinctly. The eyes shone like balls of crimson fire—an impression which, I learned later, was only gained when you looked deep and straight into them.[38]

George Maxwell, an early traveller to the Malay forests, describes a tiger hunt and the weapons used by the Malays to beat a forest.

Such men as owned, or had been able to borrow, a small dagger of a peculiar shape known as a 'golok rembau', exhibited their weapons with complacency and pride, for these daggers are supposed by the Malay to possess such extraordinary, even magical, properties that even a tiger is powerless against them.

When the local chief announced that everything was ready, an old pawang stepped forward with a bunch of twigs of a tree for which a tiger is thought to have a peculiar dread. Holding this small bundle in both hands, he repeated over it the charm known as 'that which closes the tiger's mouth,' and then, after another incantation which was intended to prevent the tiger from wounding us, proceeded to break the twigs into short fragments, which he distributed first among the shooters, and then among the beaters. The ceremony did not take long, but by the time it was over, and the final words of advice, exhortation, and command had been said on every side, the sun was strong enough to make the shade welcome; and without further delay the old chief led his picturesque throng of beaters down one path, while we set off along a track that took us into another part of the forest.

In the middle of this 'tiger beat' suddenly there was a pause. There was silence for a moment, and then a great voice shouted, 'Selawat!' (Prayer). 'Selawat!' shouted every one; and thereupon one of the men in the long line chanted aloud some verses of the Koran, concluding by shouting at the top of his voice the words of the creed of Islam: 'La' ila'hu illa' llahu; wa Muhammadu'r—rasulu' llahi' (There is no God but Allah, and Muhammad is the prophet of Allah). And from every voice in the array that was hidden up and down the forest came the roar of the response of the final Allah. Apart from its religious aspect, the use of the 'selawat' is to enable the men to know whereabouts in the denseness and tangle of the forest undergrowth the animal is hidden.

Before long the cry arose again, 'Here he is ! Here he is !' Upon this the old chief in charge of the drive shouted an order, 'Tahan, tahan !' (Steady, hold steady !) Down on a knee dropped every man of the two hundred that composed the line. Close to his side each man gripped his spear, with its point thrust upwards into the dark forest undergrowth in front of him.

The excitement by this time was almost overpowering in its intensity. I could not, of course, see the men, but knew by the sound that only this distance separated us, and that on the other side of the thickets and tree-trunks in front of me, fierce Malay eyes glared and peered for the hidden tiger. Then suddenly, in a tree half-way between the beaters and the guns, a squirrel raised its chattering note of alarm. Another squirrel immediately took up the cry, and the pair of them kept up such an incessant excited clamour that it was plain that they were scolding an intruder; it was obvious, too, that the intruder was within a few yards of them.

The nearer of the beaters heard it and dropped on their knees, with their spears thrust forward to receive it. 'Here he is ! Here he is ! Steady ! Hold steady !'

For a space not a man moved; probably not a man breathed. Then I shouted that the animal that had come out was only a pig, and that the tiger had not yet shown itself. 'Pig,' they roared up and down the line, 'only a pig'.[39]

Elsewhere Maxwell says, 'But whatever the average person's feelings may be regarding the race of cats, there is little doubt that almost every one has a peculiar sensation of the almost god-like beauty, power, activity, and strength of a tiger.'

This 'god-like beauty' and the awe its strength inspired led to a belief in the tiger's magical qualities, in were-tigers, and in tiger spirits. Another hunter, Patrick Alexander, experienced the accuracy of some of these beliefs. To shoot a man-eater in the area he had to consult the *pawang* of the village. The pawang in turn organized a ceremony to consult the spirits. A goat was sacrificed and the blood saved from coagulation. The meat was divided into three portions and cooked with rice, one for the pawang, one for the forest spirit, and one for the tiger spirit. In the night the pawang was surrounded by charms, shells and, even the clothing of the tiger's victims. The pawang offered a prayer to the lord of the heavens and the spirit of the forest seeking their permission to search for the man-eater. He ended the ceremony with a prayer to Allah.

His chanting got louder as he dropped various charms into the blood; the blood bubbled and a terrific struggle ensued between the pawang and the spirit amidst shrieks, snarls, and other animal sounds. Amidst loud cries, the pawang thrust the spirit into the glowing charcoal and collapsed in a heap.

When he opened his eyes he informed the hunter that the Forest Spirit had given permission to kill the tiger, but only after an animal with one eye missing was shot. If hot rains fell, the hunt should be stopped, otherwise a chief's son would be sacrificed.

Alexander went off the next day and encountered a wild boar, which he shot and found to his surprise, had a missing eye. Soon it started raining and a little later a snarling tiger was encountered and shot, but Alexander was paralysed to find that it had killed a chief's son who had been half devoured. He says, 'Was it coincidence again, or fate? I don't venture to explain the episode, but I know from actual records the Malay pawangs have made even more uncanny predictions which have been inexplicably fulfilled.'

In Malaysia as in Indo-China, the tiger was never referred to as *harimau* (the local name) but always respectfully called the 'striped prince' or 'old hairy face'. A tiger could hear itelf referred to as a tiger and could take this as an insult!

Locke gives an interesting example of the magical aura and reverence surrounding a tiger:

Also in the Ibok area at that time, if the reports which reached me were true, as I believe they were, was a very old male tiger with unusually long and distinctive whiskers. Age had whitened much of the hair of his face and had given him an air of great venerability, prompting the local Malays to accord to him the rank and name of Dato (Sir). As is often the case when an animal becomes noted locally for its age or size, the theory was advanced that this Dato among tigers would never be killed except by a bullet of solid silver.[40]

Locke was probably referring to what the forest communities considered as the most sacred amongst tigers—the white tiger. But tigers in general were objects of reverence: 'I have read that if a Malay comes across tiger tracks in the jungle he will cover them with leaves and a twig or two to prove that he has shown due deference to the lord of the jungle.'

The magical aura around the tiger meant that the invocation of the tiger spirit formed an integral part of treatment of any serious illness among all the communities and tribes that lived in the Malayan jungle—the Berua, the Negrito, the Semang, the Sakin or the Bemor.

The shaman would invoke the tiger spirit amidst frenzied drum-beating and dancing. Mircea Eliade analyses a Malayan séance:

The evocation of the tiger is performed for the purpose of summoning and securing the incarnation of the mythical ancestor, the first great shaman. The 'pawang' observed by Skeat did in effect turn himself into a tiger; he ran on all fours, roared and licked the patient's body for a long time as a tigress licks her cubs. The magical dances of Kelantan must include evocation of the tiger, no matter for what reason the séance has been organised. The dance culminates in the state of lupa or 'forgetfulness' or 'trance' (from

Sanskrit *lopa*, 'loss' or 'disappearance') in which the actor loses consciousness of his own personality and incarnates some spirit.

In the Kelantan area where tigers are still found, a tiger or were-tiger is supposed to appear at least once in a séance and a Kelantan shaman may refuse to hold a séance in case the tiger it attracts might get shot. The ritual of a Malay séance is elaborate and can occupy many days.

In Perak, musicians beat a one-sided drum and shriek out chants. Soon possessed by a tiger spirit, the shaman growls, spits and crawls under a mat. He dances frenziedly; sprinkling rice paste on the sufferer. The connection between the tiger, grain and fecundity is a common one throughout tiger territory.

In Selangor, a séance took place three nights running and the same odd 'number' of people participated each night. To receive the tiger spirit the shaman had an assortment of flowers, doves, and centipedes, all made of palm leaf. After possession by the tiger spirit, the shaman, besides growling and scratching, has also been known to lick the body of the naked patient. The evil spirit that is expelled in a séance is normally driven to a vessel containing food. In Kelantan and Pahang it was believed that the shamans themselves could physically turn into tigers.

Amongst the Negritos the *halak* is a man who has the ability to enter a trance or be possessed by a spirit. They believe that when a halak dies he becomes a tiger, but a tiger that will never harm his own people. Only when he has lived the life span of the tiger, will his soul enter the next world. The Malays fear the Negritos as they consider all of them to be were-tigers. The Negritos believe in two souls, one is the life spirit and the other the dream soul. When alive, the dream soul leaves the body at night and can even wander around as a tiger, capturing the excitement of the dream. After death the life spirit dies, but soon after the burial rituals are over, the dream soul journeys into another world.

Among the Negritos, the transformation from man to tiger is

supposed to occur through the medium of water. Tigers swim through lakes and rivers to turn themselves into people and even when turning back into tigers, the 'underground water' transition is essential. Sometimes magical yellow sarongs with black stripes can effect such a transition. They regard the tiger as the son of the 'Thunder God' Karei, thus connecting the tiger to water and rain, and regeneration. In China too, the tiger in conjunction with the dragon was believed to be able to create rain.

For the Negritos, the tiger is the executor of special punishments for those who sin. If proper thanks are not given for food, a tiger is said to kill the offender by creating a thunderstorm where lightning strikes the evil. Sexual activities during the day are forbidden as they anger the Thunder God Karei, who will exact punishment through the attack of a tiger.

The Batek Negritos guard their habitats with palm frond fences to protect their wandering souls from tigers who they believe will otherwise discover them with the aid of their excellent night vision.

Malay shamans tend to invoke the spirits of their ancestors who dealt with tigers. This power can be passed on to their descendents. The Malays are much more frightened of these spirit tigers than the real ones.

Be it the Semang, the Sakai, or the Bomor of Kelantan, shamanistic powers lie in the ability to invoke the tiger spirit and in this South-East Asian jungle, the tiger formed part of an 'extremely archaic religious complex'. In these areas, invocation of the tiger spirit seemed to create well-being and harmony.

In Malaysia, belief in were-tigers, human beings who can turn themselves into tigers especially at dusk, is widespread. This belief probably originates from ancient Malay legends about tigers turning themselves into men.

In the province of Negri Sembilan there is supposed to be a grave shaded by a yellow Champaka tree. The tenant of this grave was believed to attend to his widow in the form of a tiger and all through the area of Jempul there are several graves which are believed to have produced tigers from human corpses. There is the story of a visitor to a village who fell ill and vomited out feathers—the tiger man who had killed many chickens the day before—and the story of the tiger trap that trapped a man but around which there were only pugmarks of a tiger.

Deep in the interior of the jungle, there are believed to be tiger villages and tiger men who live in houses and behave like human beings. It is believed that the house posts are made of tree nettles, the roofs thatched with human hair; men's bones are the rafters and their skins house walls. These tiger men seem to live peacefully in between periodic attacks for carefully selected prey. The Malacca straits are supposed to have several of these tiger villages.

Among the population of Jempul certain families are considered tiger families. Members of these families become tigers or tigresses after death. These families are supposed to be related to certain tigers of the forest and in times of crisis, these tiger relatives come from the forest to protect cattle and poultry from other tigers, and paddy fields from the ravages of wild boar. If a member of one of these families falls ill, there is always a tiger around the house. The tiger is harmless to others and has come to express his concern at his relative's ill health. When the relative dies and the burial is over, the corpse vanishes, leaving behind the white shroud and tiger pugmarks on the ground. The corpse metamorphoses into a tiger. The tiger returns to the area and will even reveal distinguishing marks on his body similar to the ones of the man who died. Zainul Abidin Bin Ahmad records his own experience when a herd of buffaloes had entered his grandmother's compound and were destroying all the vegetables; his grandmother shouted for the help of a friend who had died a year before, and lo and behold, the angry roar of a tiger was followed by a chase and the buffaloes left, running for their lives.

The tiger *akuan* or friendly spirit could be conjured in a dream and there are many tales of a cure from illness being effected through such means. In one such case, the tiger akuan came to a seriously ill man and asked him to sleep in the open the next night. He did and the tiger came, stripped him naked, and licked his whole body with its tongue, soaking him in saliva. The man was cured a couple of days later.

Malaysia's folklore, belief and social prescriptions are rich in tiger tales. It is a common belief that a mother crocodile watches her young carefully when hatching because if one strays into the forest, it turns into a tiger. In Selangor, they believe that it becomes a monitor lizard which is regarded as the intermediary between crocodile and tiger. A Malay swears to the truth saying, 'If I lie, may a tiger seize me.' All the taboos concerning childbirth are strictly observed for it is said that if they are broken, the woman will be devoured by a tiger. No article of iron is placed near graves as its musty smell is supposed to attract tigers. When a hut is built, a fire is lit before building it. If the smoke does not rise into the sky, then a new spot is chosen because it is believed that a tiger will otherwise raze the hut to the ground. According to the Semang, if forest leeches are picked off a person and burnt outside his shelter, tigers will be attracted by the smell of the burning blood. Malays believe that a tiger never attacks human beings from the front as on the forehead of every person is inscribed a verse from the Koran proclaiming man's superiority over animals.

Elaborate ceremonies are undertaken when a tiger is killed. Supported by posts, the animal is made to look alive. Its mouth is forced open, its tongue droops outside, and a rattan is attached to its upper jaw and held by a man. The stripes are sometimes touched with charcoal to ensure that the soul does not come near them. Frenzied dances are performed around the body.

The Malay wayang siam which is the shadow theatre, also reflects the significance of the tiger in the region. A common performance is one where the forest clown gets attacked by a tiger and after a great battle subdues it but is unable to get rid of its influence; therefore he seeks the help of his master betara guru who finally 'tosses' the tiger out of the arena. This little performance at the end or beginning of the main performance underscores the master–disciple relationship.

It is only fitting that one of the rarest instances of tiger sightings is recorded from Malaysia, a land so rich in tiger lore. J.C. Moulton early in the twentieth century reported that a fisherman off the coast of Kelantan came across a dark object moving on the surface of the water. It was 5 miles from the mainland and turned out to be a fully grown tiger. It is the only record of a tiger swimming at such a distance at sea.

Locke estimated in the early 1950s that there were nearly 3000 tigers in Malaysia. With the unbridled exploitation of natural resources and clearance of forests that the latter half of the twentieth century has seen, the tiger population today in Peninsular Malaysia is estimated at 650. It could be even less. The state of Pahang has a population of 150, Trengganu 90, Kelantan 95, Perak 60, Johore 75, Kedah 20, Selangor 30, Negri Sembilan 17, and Taman Negara nearly 80.[41]

The east coast of Peninsular Malaysia is still relatively unspoilt with some remarkable beaches, and frequently hosts the giant leathery turtles which nest in the sand. These sea turtles can weigh up to a ton and the females can lay nearly 100 eggs at a time. The wilderness stretches across the South China Sea to Sabah and Sarawak with a variety of startling flowers and rich wildlife. Up in the highlands at 6000 feet can be found some of the world's largest and most spectacular butterflies. The large and extensive Taman Negara National Park straddles the rugged mountains and forests where the states of Phang, Trengganu, and Kelantan meet. The area covers nearly 1700 sq. miles.

Taman Negara is one of the world's oldest tropical forests and is home to a few hundred Negrito Pygmies who live here in complete harmony with nature.

The tiger shares this forest with the gaur, elephant, a few Sumatran rhinos, barking deer, sambar, wild pig, mouse deer, white landed gibbons, pig-tailed macaques, and banded leaf monkeys. In this area alone, 250 species of resident and migratory birds have been recorded. The tigers in Peninsular Malaysia are skilled swimmers and often in this area, a tiger can be found swimming across the Tahan River. The future of the tiger in these areas remains a pressing question mark. If such tropical forests were left to the Negritos, the tiger would surely survive.

Into Singapore

The tiger's expertise in water took it to the island of Singapore centuries ago. Here it seems to have flourished. In *Rambles of a Naturalist,* published in 1869, Cuthbert Collingwood states,

A great deal is said of the number of tigers which are supposed to infest Singapore. A recent writer estimates the deaths from these animals at 365 per annum, chiefly among Chinese cultivators of the Gambier plantations in the interior of the island. Residents at Singapore, however, always assured me that there was no danger whatever from them, and that they are never seen now.

That there are tigers in Singapore no one doubts; but while Mr Cameron supposes that there are as many as 20 couples in the island, others believe that six to eight tigers would be a sufficiently high estimate. Formerly they came much nearer to the town, but still it is long since the jungle near the plantations was infested.[42]

There is an incident of how a watchman at a plantation saw 'two eyes like glowing coals shining upon him through the darkness'.

An old guide book of the area, early last century, states that tigers were so numerous that passengers who arrived on steamers could see them at the water's edge. Collingwood wonders,

It is difficult to conceive what can induce tigers to cross over to Singapore; for although there are a few deer and plenty of pigs on the island, there is a much greater variety of game in the Johore peninsula. Can it be a taste for human flesh, which is more plentiful in the island?[43]

There can be no doubt that tigers were sighted in Singapore. Another late nineteenth-century traveller stated of the Singapore tigers: 'Tigers were abundant in these days and even entered the kitchen, so for several evenings he lay in wait for the tiger but no tiger came'.[44]

However it is not clear if tigers regularly swam back and forth across the straits, or if Singapore was settled territory for them.

Be that as it may, the tiger's influence certainly pervaded the entire straits area and even in Borneo, the only large island in the area from which there are no authentic tiger records, the forest communities believed that the tiger had existed there in old times. Once again there was a body of belief around the tiger even here. Writing in the *Journal of the Straits* in 1880, A. Hart Everett states,

When visiting the Serimbo Mountain in Sarawak in 1870 some land Dyaks voluntarily retailed to me an account of large tigers (harimau) which they had heard described by the old men of their tribe and in whose existence they themselves firmly believed.

This account agreed exactly with another which I had heard from the Balan Dyaks (Sea Dyaks) of the Semunjan River, who declared that a pair of these animals haunted a cave in the Pupok hill.[45]

Everett finally uncovered a tiger skull in a 'head house' in the beams of the roof above the fireplace in a Singgi Dyak village in Sarawak. He was unable to decipher whether it was skull or fossil, so brown was it. The Dyaks said that it had come in a dream many moons ago. Everett tried to purchase it some months later but the Dyaks refused to part with it and said that since the day he touched it they had been afflicted by heavy rain which had damaged their crops. Further, they said that someone had once broken a small bone from the skull and had been killed by lightning, and if the entire skull were removed it would cause the death of all Singgi Dyaks. The skull had to remain with the Dyaks. Everett also had reports of tigers from the Kayan of Rejang river.

Into Sumatra

The tiger moved to the islands of Indonesia long ago. The Sumatran tiger may have crossed over when the lands between the Malaccan straits were contiguous or it might have swum across.

The islands of Indonesia house volcanoes, rain forests, and thick, dark, inaccessible mangrove swamps. The royal chronicles of AD 416 state, 'The noise was fearful, at last the mountain Kapi with a tremendous roar burst into pieces and sank into the deepest of the earth—inhabitants were drowned and swept away with all their property.'

On 27 August 1883 the volcano of Krokatau exploded with such fury that its blasts were heard thousands of miles across the Indian Ocean. The waves from this island sped through Java and Sumatra. Nearly 40,000 people died in this eruption. The crew of a ship found corpses of tigers floating in the sea 140 miles from Ujung Kulan.

In the nineteenth century the island of Sumatra abounded in tigers, as an early traveller found much to his surprise,

My horse suddenly snorted in a strange manner, and came to a dead stop with its feet planted in the ground, then reared back; at the same moment the great body of a tiger shot close past my face and alighted with a heavy thud in the jungle on my other side. Haunted with the idea that I was perhaps being stalked, the night became doubly dismal to me.[46]

The Dutch colonials who took over Sumatra were so overwhelmed by the tiger's all pervading presence on the island that they tried to deal with it by shooting it in large numbers. This wanton killing was to radically affect the relationship between man and nature that existed on the island.

Describing the forests of Sumatra early this century, Ton Schilling says in *Tigermen of Anai,*

When you make acquaintance for the first time with the primeval forest in all its disarray, you will be struck by its green uniformity. Every tree will seem like every other: the trees are surrounded by thousands, millions of others of the same species, enormous giants with perpendicular trunks, rising as pillars to bear the thick leafy roof, a green cathedral. The sunlight penetrates only through occasional small gaps in the leafage. The ground is soft and spongy from the moist and oozy humus, which gives off an odour of damp and decay. Where the sunlight falls, the dry leaves and twigs rustle and snap as you pass.

Under the vast dome, lianas hang in great curves, bearing thick bunches of leaves. Dense undergrowth hampers your passage and the rotting trunks of fallen trees lie across your path. And all is green, green in a thousand shades, with a nerve-racking absence of any relief.

So it is at first. But when you have become more familiar with the forest you will learn to notice small breaks in the monotony on which the eye can gratefully dwell—a tree almost buried under a dense drapery of moss, a rattan liana garlanded with flaming red orchids, or a thick clump of bracken with a woodcock's nest.

As soon as the depression produced at first by the ubiquitous greens has passed away and you have grown accustomed to the environment, this adventure of penetrating the primeval forest becomes absorbing, and you make the discovery of an astonishing life, full of variety. Often eyes and ears are unable to cope with all this beauty.[47]

Schilling closely encountered tigers in the jungles of Ranalinggau in the Palembang district and in fact became as accustomed to one tiger family's presence in his grounds as if they were domestic cats.

Suddenly I was startled out of a weary semi trance by the Mandur's grip of my arm and his excited whisper, 'Thuan-harimau!'

On the right, in the dark by the bamboos, gleamed the eyes of a big tiger; nearer the entrance two cubs were playing round the recumbent tigress. It would have been a pretty picture in a zoo, seen beyond good strong bars, but I could only feel a thrill of horror. And the next night 'Thuan Thuan.' I jumped out of bed, picked up my gun, turned up the lamp and hurried into the dining room.

The tigers were there again. The biggest one was lying on the edge of the enclosure and the cubs were jumping about.

The tigress stood with her head erect and her tail stretched out, and her eyes fixed on the servants. My heart beat violently as I raised my gun. I was about to shoot but something seemed to hold me back. The tigers were doing nobody any harm.

On moonlit nights I saw them playing in the enclosure, innocently and good humouredly like great cats. Gradually I got used to them. The tigers never did the slightest harm: on the contrary, they did me a great service, for now when I was unable to get back at night no thief ever ventured anywhere near my house.[48]

Schilling goes on to describe the reactions of the forest communities to this happening:

At kampong festivals, presents of food were sent to me. The people kept me supplied with all sorts of good things—fruit, eggs and river fishes. They greeted me almost reverently as I passed them. In short, I was treated like a prince, though I was a very ragged one, with my patched khaki clothes and clay-soiled hobnailed boots.[49]

The tiger family arrived to play and rest nearly every day and Schilling watched them grow over a period of months. It all changed when a guest unsuccessfully attempted to shoot one of the tigers. After that the tigers never came back.

According to Schilling, in Sumatra there was widespread belief in human beings who are able to change themselves into tigers, referred to as *vngelmu-gadongan* or tigermen. These people seemed totally normal except that they lacked the groove in the upper lip. People in Peninsular Malaysia and in Sumatra believed that somewhere deep in the forests of Sumatra, amidst the Jambi highlands of Mt Dempo lived the Korinchi and that all these people had the capacity to change into tigers and vice-versa, and their villages were referred to as tiger villages. At dusk they turned into tigers, at dawn into human beings, and such transformations took place in water as man and tiger both enjoy bathing in water, which in a way is the essence of life. The tiger was regarded as the son of the Thunder God. These tiger kingdoms of Korinchi were like soul villages where people who might have died similar deaths gathered together and lived sometimes as tigers, sometimes as human beings.

In Aceh too it was believed that certain people could suddenly transform themselves into tigers especially when a member of their families had for some reason been killed by a tiger. The intensity of the loss could suddenly cause the surviving family member to sprout fur and claws, after which he would rush into the forest. His return to humanity was only possible when he was rolled in a special cloth. These magical powers were confined to certain families that retained an integral affinity with the tiger.

The Batak would never kill the tiger, believing that the souls of their ancestors resided in the tiger. Tiger flesh was taboo among them. It was believed that members of the clan were either descended from tigers or their souls could transmigrate into tigers since they were all linked by their ancestors.

Tigers were believed to reside near tombs, but visible only to people who had not infringed or sinned. Royalty, nobility, and courageous warriors claimed descent from the white tiger, and the grave of the former sultan of Aceh is supposed to be guarded by a white tiger that appears on Thursdays to receive offerings and grant requests.

In Daya it was held that the grave of a hero was guarded by two black tigers.

Islam in the region too, betrays the tiger's influence. The graves of Muslim holy men were believed to be guarded by tigers. All important mystics and others who were intensely revered had white tigers as grave guardians.

When anyone transgressed the rules of Islam, Allah, it was said, executed punishment through the tiger. Even when 100 people died in 1951 in tiger attacks near Bengkulu on the south-west coast of Sumatra, no tiger was ever held responsible as it was held to be the revenge of Allah. It was widely believed that the killing of tigers could cause havoc in the form of floods, volcanic eruptions, natural disaster, or accidents. The tiger only devoured those who had committed evil deeds.

The Sumatran legend about the origin of the tiger establishes man as the father of the tiger. A newly-wed couple were making love in their hut in the middle of a rice field. The man was about to climax when they heard someone approaching. He withdrew while ejaculating and some of the sperm fell on the earth. It turned into a tiger and went into the forest.

It was commonly believed in Sumatra that the tiger did not bother man unless man bothered it; the few tigers that raided villages had been banished by their own societies. They were unable to return to being normal tigers in a forest as they would be chased out by the forest tiger.

In Daya there used to be a ritual feast where several water buffaloes were slaughtered and offered to the tiger so that he may protect the pepper plantations and rice fields. After this ritual meal, the tiger would become protector of their crops against other animals and there were few worries till harvest time. Wednesday was a tiger holiday, a day when the tiger would enter the village of which he was guardian. He would only bother those who had wronged him. On this day of the tiger very few people worked; those who did could meet with an accident. Tigers and tiger spirits would also guard water buffaloes against the raids of banished tigers.

There are many stories in Sumatra of tigers helping lost men or women in a forest by bringing them food for survival. Stories also exist of men and women helping tigers by providing them with food, and even burying them when needed.

The Gayo of Sumatra call the tiger the grandfather of the forests and for the Kubu, the tiger is their best friend. In Minangkabau, if the tiger had to be trapped, the process would be accompanied by prayers in Arabic, bamboo flute music, and tiger-capturing songs that might entice the tiger into the cage.

The shamans of this island invariably invoked the spirit of the tiger and were considered as having the ability to turn into tigers. In Aceh, a shaman candidate had to suck the tongue of a dead shaman before draping himself in a striped tiger-like cloth after which water was poured on to the dead shaman's body and then soaked on to the prospective shaman. The shaman was depicted as herding flocks of tigers rather than buffaloes.

Blood, urine, or saliva were considered powerful in locating souls. When offerings were made to the spirit of the tiger, if these were mixed with spit, it was like adding a bit of oneself to it. In Aceh, tiger milk was considered a special medicine; a bit of tiger skin, tooth, or nail was vital as protection while travelling. The link with the tiger is visible even in the art of self-defence which is called *silat minangkabau* and traditionally practised over much of Sumatra. It is based on the movements of the tiger and the master who taught this art was said to be related to the tiger.

When the Dutch East India Company arrived in Sumatra, the island was filled with tigers, but as has already been mentioned, they couldn't deal with this and resorted to large-scale killing of the tigers by having them declared as pests. Thousands of tigers were killed.

In 1978 the eight provinces of Sumatra had nearly 1000 tigers. Today the population has gone down to 300–700 tigers. Most of the tigers are found in Aceh, Jambi, Sumatra, Selatan, and Bengkulu. With large-scale logging operations under way, the tiger may be forced to retreat to the mountainous regions. The future of the tiger is under threat once again as the man–tiger link has been snapped.

Into Java

Across a few miles of sea from Sumatra is the land of the Javan tiger, which is regarded as the smallest of tigers. On this island, Pleistocene fossils of the tiger have been found. An early traveller writes of Java in the late nineteenth century:

Especially in the centre of the island there are tigers whose ravages are still considerable. Lightning and tigers are the two greatest terrors of the Javanese: he speaks of them only with fearful respect; their victims amount to hundreds each year, yet the natives abstain from any systematic campaign against the tigers, despite the terror which they inspire, because the destruction of the tigers results, in their experience, in the advent of herds of wild pigs which ruin the crops.[50]

In a way tiger, man, and forest were united in a close relationship affording each other mutual protection. Man was dissuaded by fear of the tiger from cutting down too much forest, and the forest concealed the tiger from the hunter. The tiger protected forest communities from the ravages of other wild animals and the forest provided them sustenance.

In Gumpul in West Java, the spirit of a prince is supposed to have taken the form of a white tiger and guarded the people of the surrounding area. The Sundanese regarded were-tigers of nobles and princes as protective spirits who continued to rule and keep a link between past and present. They also felt that a special wood from the Kaboa tree found between west and central Java had the power to invoke an ancestral tiger.

Since the souls of the ancestor resided in the tiger, even the raising of animals with striped or spotted fur was prohibited. Blood was considered a powerful locater of the soul and if a man-eater was killed by a hunter, the family which had lost someone to the tiger would attempt to bathe in the tiger's blood, so that the tiger's soul could become a part of the person.

In Java, tigers and buffaloes were both considered powerful and there are records in the middle of the last century of fights being organized between the two for the entertainment of nobles, princes, and agents of the Dutch East Indies. Tigers were captured from the forest and kept captive till the fight. The buffalo was usually able to overcome the tiger who tried to leave the arena, but was confronted by a ring of men with spears and usually died; but if he escaped he was allowed to return to the forest. Much ritual and worshipping of the tiger preceded his release into the arena. It does seem strange that although the tiger was such an object of reverence in Java and Sumatra, such fights were organized; it is worth exploring whether they originally took place only on rare occasions and whether these accelerated after the arrival of the Dutch.

Schilling describes his experiences of the Javan tiger early in the twentieth century:

Minute after minute passed without anything happening. Those minutes seemed to us eternities—eternities of the utmost nervous tension. Our eyes burned as we strained them in searching the edge of the reeds. We knew that the faint moonlight was shining straight into our pupils and therefore was almost closing our eye-lids.

Suddenly we heard behind us the snapping of a dry twig. Without noticing anything, the tiger had passed along the reed-field and was now behind us. This was unexpected, and an unpleasant situation. It was now essential that at least one of us should turn round, but that was almost impossible without making a noise. It had to be done, therefore, as slowly and cautiously as possible, I turned my head round millimetre by millimetre, but I could not turn it far enough to see in the right direction. Meanwhile I had the unpleasant feeling down my back that the tiger was watching us from behind, at the moment perhaps only in curiosity, but perhaps also calculating whether it could leap up to our platform.

I listened intently for any fresh noise, but all was quiet. So fierce was the beat of my blood in my temples that it seemed to me that the tiger must hear it. Suddenly I was streaming with perspiration.

It seemed an eternity before we heard any further sound from the tiger. This time it was an impatient snarl, again exactly behind us. My nerves were so strained that the noise seemed like a thunderclap.[51]

And finally, 'Suddenly I realised that I was looking at the tiger's eyes. Uncertainly and deceptively there gleamed two greenish, spectral eyes in the darkness. They disappeared and then came back into view, remained awhile and disappeared again'.[52]

The Javan tiger today is extinct but it lives on in myth, legend, ritual, and belief. The traditional shadow theatre of Java is one place where the tiger lives on as the guardian of the tree of life.

Into Bali

A few miles across the sea from Java on the small island of Bali, which was the end of the tiger's domain, the smallest of its sub-species, the Balinese tiger was to be found. It is extinct today and probably became extinct in 1937 though there have been reports of tigers in the 1950s and even until 1975 when residents of north-west Bali thought they had seen a tiger. It was during the two World Wars that large-scale hunting by Dutch colonials sealed the tiger's fate. The tiger from Bali has long gone and what is left are narratives of early travellers at the beginning of the twentieth century, 'The fauna is not so rich as that of Java, the rhinoceros and banteng no longer exist, but numbers of tigers roam the west and centre of the island.'

But the tiger continues to play a significant part in Balinese folklore wherein it is said to have a connection with God Brahma; Goddess Pulaki is still followed by three tigers who have the power to possess men. The Barong which is a mythical Balinese beast, sometimes has the form of a tiger and is depicted draped in scarlet material with stylized stripes.

Belief in were-tigers was widespread in Bali. The Leyak of Bali were said to feed on corpses which could change their physical form and transform them into tigers. These were-tigers were distinguished by the absence of the groove on the upper lip. In Lombok when there was unrest in the past, Balinese soldiers were said to have created fear by changing into tigers.

It is unfortunate that the powerful outsiders who were to have such a far-reaching influence in the region rarely had the sensitivity to appreciate the deep-rooted links between man and nature, and man and tiger in particular.

Ton Schilling was one of the few that did. He says of the Balinese people's beliefs:

I have told you of some of the strange things in the wilderness that continually fill the life there with new surprises. It makes a difference to a man's life there how he treats these things, whether he takes them at all seriously or dismisses them at once with a skeptical smile. The people of the wilderness are alienated by the latter attitude and become taciturn when faced with it; but if one is ready to listen to them without any show of prejudice one will hear many things about the life in the virgin forests that reveal a realm full of beauty and happiness.[53]

Unfortunately most of the world dismissed these cultures and beliefs, with little tolerance for an alternate wisdom and way of being.

From my knowledge of tigers and their incredible ability to swim, it seems quite possible that they could have crossed from Sumatra to Java and especially from Java to Bali—a distance of only 1.5 miles. The question then of sub-species would really have to be re-examined. But whether sub-species or not, this was certainly the land of the sea tiger. There is no question, however, that tiger and man in these Indonesian islands have shared a deep affinity. Having travelled with the tiger through from Siberia down to the Indonesian islands, let us follow the tiger into some of the areas where it branched off.

Into Burma

From southern China and Indo-China, the tiger found its way into Burma, what is today known as Myanmar. It is believed to have entered Burma after the last Ice Age. As in other parts of its domain, among the Burmese forest people too the tiger had a very important place. A tattoo of a tiger on the leg was supposed to provide courage. There were villages in Burma early this century which were considered tiger villages, and all the people in these villages had the ability to turn into tigers and vice versa. The Tamans of Burma did this by urinating on the ground and then rolling around naked on that wet patch.

The first descriptions of the tiger in Burma come from the British in 1859. By this time, Burma and India were completely colonized.

The time was 1859. The scene was the forest-covered hilly ground about seventy miles north of Moulmein, in what is now Bilin Township of Thaton

district, Burma, between the Sittang and Salween rivers. A detachment of
the 32nd Madras Native infantry, under Captain Manley, was marching on
business there, going in single file along a footpath, proceeded by the civil
officer with them, a Mr Charles Hill.

Suddenly Hill came upon a tiger lying full length on the footpath apparently
asleep. He looked round and called for his gun. It was for the moment out
of reach.

The few seconds Hill stood waiting for a gun would seem as many
minutes, or more. In short it is easy to imagine how, as he watched the big
beast, perhaps stretching itself and yawning, seeming likely to step aside
soon, before a gun arrived, into a wood where a few steps would make it
safe from pursuit, the big strong man lost patience, and lifting his stick
with hands he hit the tiger on the head between the eyes.[54]

The tiger finally escaped, but even in 1891 the Burmese referred to
Hill as *Kya-ma-haing* or 'the man the tiger did not beat'.

But there were few such escapes for the tiger in Burma. From
1928 to 1938, Burma lost nearly 2000 tigers, killed by 'any method
of hunting and in unlimited numbers'.

Between British colonization and Burmese politics, the tiger was
wiped out along with large parts of its forest. There could still be a
few hundred tigers in these areas but to the world they are invisible.
From Burma the tiger reached India.

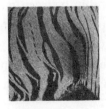

Into India

Encompassing what is now Bangladesh and the eastern regions, the
tiger spread throughout India—north, west, south, east. Leaving
Burma it entered the land of the Nagas. Like the Chinese who believed

in layers of skies, one above the other, the Nagas believe that the earth has a series of flat surfaces, the bottom of the nearest being the sky, and that beneath the earth lies the land of the dead into which the sun and moon set at night to bring light. An eclipse is explained as an attempt by a tiger to eat the moon or the sun, and in such situations, the crescendo of drums is supposed to halt the tiger in its attempt. Obviously here, as elsewhere, the tiger was vested with a very high level of power and ability.

The Rengma Nagas believe that the mother of the first spirit, the first tiger, and the first man came out of the earth from a Pangolin's hole. A popular myth has it that man and tiger are brothers, one in human shape, the other striped. One stayed at home, the other went to live in the forest, but one day when they met in the forest, they were forced to fight and the man tricked the tiger into crossing a river and then killed it with a poisoned dart. The tiger's body floated downstream, where it got caught in the reeds. The God Dingu-Aneni saw that the bones had come from a human womb and sat for ten years on them and hundreds of tigers were born, some to stay in the hills, others to move into the plains. Once again, existed the belief in the 'humanness' of the tiger and the 'tigerness' of man, a belief common throughout the tiger's domain.

Knowledge of Naga ritual and belief concerning the tiger comes to us through anthropologists and colonialists in the early twentieth century after the relationship between man and tiger had already been badly disturbed, especially by the large-scale slaughter of the tiger that occured under colonial rule.

Naga folklore held that the tiger was invoked as guardian of an area to successfully allow man and woman to copulate and create 'seed and fruit'.

Oaths were taken with a tiger's tooth or over a skull. Amongst the Ao Nagas, the shaman or medicine man asked for the assistance of the tiger spirits for a cure, and the Aos believed that somewhere on a high peak there lived a king of tigers and that all tiger spirits gathered regularly to propitiate this king.

The concept of were-tigers was prevalent among the Aos and there were said to be many instances when tigers were shot or injured and their human forms in a nearby village would suddenly find themselves with the same injuries. Let us look at a colonial record of such a case replete with rational Western intolerance.

This was an Ao named Imtong Lippa of Changki. While this 'beat' was going on three miles away, he was behaving like a lunatic in the house of one of the hospital servants at Mokokchung. During his possession he identified himself with one of the tigers being hunted and stated that one of them was wounded and speared.[55]

It so happened that he was accurate in his entire account of the hunt told from a tiger's point of view.

The western Rengma Nagas claimed to know of many tiger men who would reveal a variety of scars on their bodies which reflected corresponding wounds on their tigers. What the effect of the relentless hunting of tigers by the British leaving many tigers wounded, must have been on such tiger men, is to be wondered at.

Many tiger clans and tiger villages existed in this area. The Hnaihlew clan of Saiko was one such where the tiger was shown immense reverence, and it was considered a sin to injure it. The founder of this clan was supposed to have a great friend who was a tiger and who provided much help to him. Even today, sacrifices are offered to the tiger in the form of a pig and cakes of flour. These are placed on the road outside the village. If the offering is accepted, it is considered very lucky but if the tiger has walked around without eating anything, ill luck is foretold.

The Angami Nagas believed that the waters of a certain spring could change man into a tiger. The tiger for the Angami was a part of the family. Amongst the Lakhers, the man who killed a tiger would dress up like a woman and dance around the tiger's head, hair flowing down, smoking a woman's pipe, and with a spindle and thread in his hand! Perhaps it is suggestive of the earth mother, reproductivity, and regeneration.

The Nagas never speak directly of the tiger and even if a man is killed by one, it is only said that he was devoured in the jungle.

Tigers seem to have been killed by the Nagas on ceremonial and ritual occasions only. They were normally caught in traps but could also be surrounded and speared. However, unlike the trophy hunters of the West, few boasted of the deed and amongst the Rengma Nagas they would say, 'The village killed a tiger.' Ceremonies, rituals and strict taboos about cutting, skinning, and eating the flesh followed the tiger's death. The cut head was often put in a stream of water so that the spirit or the Tiger God would not seek revenge, or the mouth was wedged open to allow the release of the tiger's spirit. The Lhota Nagas put leaves in the tiger's mouth for the same purpose. The Lephori kept their tigers' heads in trees and used them for oath-taking.

The tiger quickly spread throughout India, moving into the mangrove swamps, evergreen forests, dry deciduous forests, and the variety of other vegetation that covered Indian land. There must have been 50,000–80,000 tigers roaming India in the nineteenth century, adjusting to different temperatures and climates.

The earliest depictions of the tiger on the Indian subcontinent go back to Harappan seals dating to 2500 BC. Sometimes the tiger is horned and is seen standing with a trough-like object in front of him. On another seal is an intriguing figure, the hind portion of which is that of a tiger and the front portion that of a woman; the woman has a conspicuous long plait and a tree growing above her head. Another seal depicts a nude female, upside down with thighs held wide apart, with two tigers standing on one side. The ritual significance is not clear but evidently it evokes a feminine connection of the tiger with either fertility or birth.

Pupul Jayakar in her interpretation of the Harappan seals states the following in relation to the image of the tiger.

The earth is the great yoni. The woman's body in the Indus Valley seal is the earthbound root, the fecundating source. The arms of the inverted figure are stretched to touch the knees as in the Yogasanas (Yoga postures). The rampant tigers, guardians of initiation, protect the mysteries and the immense magic of creation. The tigers are separated from the Earth Mother by the Indus Valley script, a mantra or dharini of protection.[56]

Describing a series of three seals she states,

A ritual scene that repeats itself in endless variations on the seals of Mohenjo-Dara and Harappa is the spirit of the tree in mysterious dialogue with the tiger.

The tiger stands below the tree, motionless, in a still moment of listening. His head is turned to face the figure within the tree, to catch the sound of the rustling leaf.

In a continuing dialogue with the tiger, the lady on the tree appears on another seal; the tiger, grown to the size of the tree, listens. Two people are shown tearing out a tree each by its roots. They are bent backwards like bows, by their exertion. From between the uprooted trees, from the lacerated earth, springs a figure, the spirit of the earth, young, naked and lithe.

In the next seal the tree-woman has separated from the tree. The tree, in rhythm with the body of the woman, bends to release her. The tree-woman has undergone transformation and metamorphosis. The linear bodiless form has given place to a rounded woman's body. The virgin breasts are clearly visible. She is now half-woman, half-buffalo. Her head is crowned with horns, she has buffalo hoofs and a tail. The body of the buffalo-woman bends forward, one arm stretched to touch and claim the tiger. The other arm is curved and upraised. The great tiger of a thousand-fold energy has sprung into movement. A magical figure of powerful potency, he wears two widespread horns but they are formed like sprays of neem leaves. His chest is leaf-shaped and so are his paws.

Tiger-like is the amulet made of herbs, a saviour, a protector against hostile schemes. The forelegs of the tiger are raised. The expression has changed, the listening has given way to action. The leaf-formed tiger roars, filling the rustling forest with sound. The tree, the lady-lady and the tiger have established contact. They move in rhythm in that still moment of magic. The movement of mutation has commenced.

In the last seal of the series, the tiger and the woman have become one. The tree-buffalo-woman retains her horns. She stands erect with a long pigtail, her arms stretched sideways, her waist curved indicating flesh and substance. From the spine, at an angle to the standing figure, springs the tiger marked with stripes. The massive body of the tiger has now assumed the fragile, linear elegance of the lady on the tree. It is the lady who lifts her head and rides the tiger. The tree has disappeared. Its place on the seal has been taken by a mysterious diagram. The mutation is complete.

The importance and power of this series of seals and the mysterious relationship of the lady to the tiger is revealed in a continuing tradition at Kalibangan, where the horned-lady, the tree and the tiger appear on a seal as an almost identical composition and in another seal where the tiger and the lady have merged into a composite form.

The quality of listening and of silence, in which sounds of vast forests are contained, is the clue to the woman and the tiger seals of transformation. The form of the tree, the long-armed gesture of the women, the posture of the tiger and the stillness of the wild and fierce animals of the forest, imparts a fluidity, a dimension that dissolves barriers and prepares the ground for metamorphosis. The magical nature of plants and their capacity to initiate the spiral of transformation is suggested in the horns of the tiger which are formed of sprouting leaves and in the tendrils and leaf patterns that form his body. He who wears this para (leaf) amulet becomes a tiger, becomes a lion, becomes a bull.

There is a Chenchu tale of a woman who turned herself into a tiger— proof that she was adept at the secret rites of metamorphosis. While a tiger, she killed and ate her own baby. When the mantra to turn her back into a human form was recited and ashes sprinkled, she remained half-woman, half-tiger, the eating of human flesh having destroyed the potency of the spell. Is the half-woman, half-tiger of the Indus Valley seal an image of such an ancient belief? Are the vast numbers of the isomorphic images of composite forms of man and animal the expressions of magical acts of metamorphosis?

Separated by five thousand years, an amulet worn by primitive people who dwell on the banks of the Narmada River depicts a woman riding a tiger. The body of the tiger and the skirt that covers the body of the goddess are leaf-formed. Plants sprout around the luminous, uprising presence. The arms of the lady are outstretched in the all-including sacred gesture of the goddess. The arms are tendrils, sprouting and extending from the trunk of the body. The fragile nature of the tiger-lady, the interchangeability of plant, animal and human, the outstretched arms embracing the cosmos, affirm the mighty roots of the visual tradition. In Indian myth it is always the lady who rides the tiger.

An archaic symbol of great power, it personifies the goddess in her primitive, magical form before she is absorbed into Brahmanic theology and abandons the tiger for the lion. The symbol of the two beasts illuminates the nature of she who mounts their bodies. On the tiger the lady is potent with magic and mystery. On the lion the goddess is the benign protectress.

The tiger is not known to the singers of the Rig Vedic hymns, the lion does not appear on the Indus Valley seals. Amongst forest shrines of the Bhils of Gujarat, there is a wooden palia, a menhir pillar in the shape of a two-armed woman riding a tiger. Clay offerings of horse, bull and tiger are made to her. Her image suggests the Puranic goddess Amba or Durga. The Bhils refer to her as Hura Pura, the old ancestress. The lady astride the tiger appears also in several tribal metal icons from Mandla in Madhya Pradesh. In the Matsya Purana there is a legend wherein Brahma, pleased with the tapasya of Parvati, grants her a boon. She asks that the tiger be chief of her ganas as Vyaghrapada.

There is in Tamil Nadu a legend that Subramaniam, the son of Siva and the forest mother, loved an aboriginal virgin, Valli. To win her love he turned himself into a vengai. Vengai is the Tamil word for tiger, it is also the name of the neem tree in its male aspect before it flowers. The association of both the male neem tree as well as the tiger with Subramaniam is of great interest. Is the Indus Valley virgin, the tiger and the neem tree an illustration of an ancient legend, memories of which survive in the Subramaniam story? In ancient magic, the tiger is the guru of initiation. In the great birth seal, he guards the mysteries. In the Indus Valley pictographs the tiger is never visualized as violent, he never kills. His role is protective. He is in communion with the energy source of nature. The horned tiger is familiar in Baiga myth. When the Baiga Gunia calls on all the tigers of the world by name, the 'horned bagh' is one of them. The tiger is a phallic symbol of the wildness and grandeur of the virile, heroic male. The Atharva Veda refers to the tiger as the first of all creatures. In Nepal, Bhairava is worshipped in the image of a tiger.

In the seal from Mohenjo-Daro, a man stands erect, arms outstretched, holding apart two rampant tigers. At Jambudvipa in Panchmari there is a cave-painting depicting a similar subject. Here the hero stands erect, taut with power and majesty, and out of his body emerge, on either side, two leaping tigers. The rampant tails of the tigers are held tautly by the magician–priest. Are these also representative of ancient magicians, who, like the Baiga priest, have special intimacy and control over tigers, who have the power to summon them from the forest, to catch them by the ear and whisper to them their secrets, and the capacity to transform themselves into tigers at will?

The magician–priests of primitive man, the Gunias and the Bhopas, draw their authority from great antiquity. They claim power over the potency of bridegrooms, the malevolence of witches, and the ferocity of tigers. Their magic is derived from the original guru-preceptor Nanga Baiga, whom the Baiga name the first magician. A myth recounts Nanga Baiga's pact with the tigers, by virtue of which only he could bind their mouths. As the Baiga or magician–priest drives iron nails into trees to guard the boundaries of the village from the influx of the terrible man-eater, he calls on his ancestor Nanga Baiga. To do this the Gunia makes two images, one of papa or sin, the other of vanaspati, the plant, the symbol of the Earth Goddess. He then calls on all the tigers by name. 'The white sheet-bagh, the horned singh-bagh, latariabagh, the hyena, jalaria-bagh, the cattle-eating dhor-bagh, kowachi-bagh, the leopard, bundia-bagh, gul-bagh, the small dorcha-bagh, the tiny dog-like bhusur-bagh, bandhia-bagh, the tail-less bunchi-bagh, the small-eared tajia-bagh, the magic wooden khunta-bagh, the tendua-bagh, the panther, Chita-bagh and son elitti-bagh. A man in the audience is filled with the spirit of the bagh and devours the image of sin. The Baiga then drives a nail into four trees to guard the four quarters of the village and invokes the images of vanaspati as Dharti Mata, the Earth Goddess, informing her that henceforth Nanga Baiga has fixed the boundaries of the village and made it safe from tigers. The antiquity of these rites is manifest in an identical spell, an Atharvan charm, to bind the mouths of tigers. The jaw, O tiger! that thou shuttest together, thou shalt not open up; that which thou openest up, thou shalt not shut together.[57]

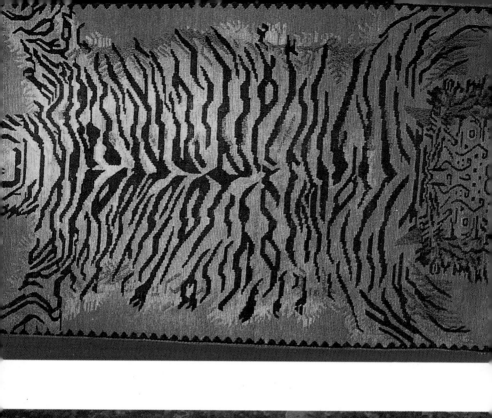

The Worli tribals live north of Mumbai in Maharashtra on tracts of land along the border of Gujarat. They practise subsistence agriculture using the slash-and-burn methods of cultivation and very rarely do they use fertilizers, believing that the earth has her own method of fertilizing herself and man-made fertilizers only cause land to turn barren. Like most other tribals in India, their relationship with nature comprises giving and taking without any overexploitation.

They have lived under Hindu, Muslim, Portuguese, Maratha, and British rule each contracting their rights over the forest as civilization encroached. In 1841 the British imposed a ban on the tribals and their use of wood, creating a severe setback in their natural rhythmn. Instead, the thickly wooded areas in which the Worlis lived became sources of timber for the British for making wooden railway sleepers.

Today the Worlis live in the rugged ranges and foothills around Thane district, still keeping a distance from the outside world. Known for their remarkable skill in painting, depicting different elements of nature, their use of geometrical shapes seems to connect them to the earliest rock and cave painters of central India, dating to 3000 BC. Worli paintings are indicative of their deep links with the tiger and it is significant that the tiger is often represented as if it were a natural part of village life, sitting or walking by with a harmless, friendly look— much like the tiger in reality. The Worli tribals believe in the Tiger God and carved wooden statues of the tiger can be found all over the Worli villages.

The Worlis believe that each 'New Year' is born at the time of the rains and as the seasons change, different gods are propitiated and one of them is the Tiger God or Vagha deva. Offerings are made to him soon after harvest, and at the time of Diwali.

The *utare bhagat* is the Worli priest or medicine man who invokes the spirit of the Tiger God for cure and healing. With deforestation, the utare bhagats have a limited role today due to their inability to find the right traditional herbs for medicinal uses. The word 'bhagat', priest or medicine man, may be derived from *baghaut* or a man who is actually a tiger. When the bhagat is possessed, the most vital form of possession is that by Vagha deva or the Tiger God who represents all that is powerful and potent and guards the village from any form of danger.

The statue of Vagha deva is found on the boundaries of villages and is a connecting link between all the tribes of the Thane area. Just before and during Diwali, the Worlis are absorbed in song and dance mainly to the tune of the *tarpa*. This period seems to start as the earth produces new plants in the harvested fields, and the joy and festivity culminates with the worship of the Tiger God after Diwali in the month of November. The tarpa, which is a phallic-shaped protruding instrument, and its tunes end at the worship of the Tiger God, seemingly to indicate what must be the most fertile and reproductive period for both the earth and the human being. It is only the young people who dance to the tarpa. As Yashodhara Dalmia puts it, it is a moment where 'the dancers merged with the darkness, soft, damp and sensuous, and only the stamp of dancing feet could be heard. At last they were free, unwatched, lost in oblivion in the very womb of nature itself'.[58]

Besides all the household gods that are worshipped, probably the most vital worship is that of the gods that look after the fields and the villages, i.e. the heroic ancestor gods responsible for warding off evil, protecting the fields, and providing better fertility and productivity for the crops. The installation of these guardian figures is accompanied by elaborate rituals undertaken by the utare bhagats who represent the Tiger God.

The Tiger God is known as Vaghya, Vagha deva, or Gama deva and is worshipped after the harvest but before threshing begins. This is followed by a worship of the crop. The Tiger God is regarded as the chief god and only after his worship can the family gods be propitiated.

The Tiger God has to be worshipped before the worship of the Mother Goddess or Earth Mother, and this is vital as the tiger is regarded as the vehicle of the Earth Mother. The Worlis believe that worshipping the tiger will protect their cattle as well as themselves from tigers. No one undertakes a journey without asking the tiger to protect the village and resolve any problem that may arise.

Sometimes a roof with four pillars can form the 'temple' of this god. His imprints in a rice field are auspicious and the Worlis believe that the 'doer of the world' has come. They say, 'He is the greatest of all gods. The others are there because of him.' When people see such an imprint, they break a coconut and smear the place with *gulal* (red lead powder). Then the fields prosper—once more the tiger's connection with fertility. Most of the images of the Tiger God are coated with *sindur*, signifying its extreme sanctity.

The festival of the Tiger God is held in the second fortnight of November, when all members of the village donate money from their harvests to propitiate the tiger. His image is surrounded by the sun, moon, stars, and trees, amidst which there could be a serpent entwined—all symbolizing life, and its endless regeneration. The propitiation of the tiger continues over three nights and days with a complicated series of rituals and the continuous invocation of the spirit of the tiger. Goats can also be sacrificed while the bhagats communicate with the tiger. It is after this worship that the propitiation of the Corn Goddess can commence.

The link between the Corn Goddess and the Tiger God dates back to olden times, and in a seventeenth-century silver amulet found in Maharashtra, she rides the tiger, her body formed of a leaf and merging with the striped leaves of a tiger. The arms of the goddess extend like branches from the trunk of the body, symbolic of the fusion between man, animal, and nature. The Tiger God is interlinked to everything, especially the Corn Goddess and thus fertility, and amongst the Worli tribals this can be linked to pregnancy and the regeneration of life.

Even in marriage, the bridal couple wears shawls which are red and yellow resembling the skin of the tiger, and draped in these shawls they visit the temple to propitiate the goddess after marriage. If the marriage goddess Palaghata is angry, the shawl can turn into a real tiger and devour the couple.

The Tiger God is the companion of Palaghata, the goddess of marriage, and he is the first spirit to be invoked during the marriage ceremony, followed by the family gods, and finally again by the Tiger God. The bhagat who gets possessed by the Tiger God during the marriage ritual is offered a chicken, and many chickens are sacrificed to obtain sanctity for the marriage from the Tiger God. During the ceremony the *umbar* tree is vital, and a branch of this tree and the Tiger God have to be married before the couple can be united. It is wood from this tree that covers the couple during the ceremony.

The colours that are used during the marriage ceremony are red for blood, yellow for corn and white for rice but once again these colours symbolizing fertility are linked to the colours of the tiger.

The tiger is the carrier of both bride and bridegroom. Such all-pervading connections with the tiger were and in some cases still are a facet of life among many different forest communities all over India. The tiger was an integral part of their way of life, their culture, their wisdom, and their spirituality.

W. Crooke in his book on the folklore in northern India published nearly a century ago, relates how the community of gardeners in Akola would never inform the hunter of the presence of tigers in their plantations, as they believed that the garden plot loses its fertility when a tiger is killed. In those days when tiger flesh was available, it was burnt to prevent disease in cattle and to destroy any blight that might affect crops. In Kolhapur, a figure of a tiger made of dry sugar-cane leaves is kept at conspicuous places in the fields to provide protection for sugar-cane crops.

A mixture of tiger whiskers with sacred grass and red lead was considered exceedingly valuable to children immediately after birth and was supposed to prevent infant mortality.

The Baghel Rajputs claim descent from the tiger and will never harm the animal. The Bhils, the Bajrawat Rajputs, and the Santhals also claim descent from the tiger. Bageshwar, the tiger deity, is very important among the Mirzapur forest communities, while *kisans* in

Mirzapur worship the tiger as Banraja or lord of the jungle. The Kurkus of Hoshangabad worship the tiger godling 'Bagh deo' who is the Wagh deo of Berar. At Petri in Berar there is a special altar dedicated to Waghai Devi, the Tiger Goddess. Legend has it that a Gond woman was seized by a tiger and then vanished completely and since then the altar to this Tiger Goddess receives frequent offerings.

The Gonds are divided into different clans or *gotras* and one of the clans—Vagmareuicka—derives its name from the tiger. The legend surrounding its origins goes thus: A tiger spared a woman who was pregnant and instead took her home and looked after her. The tiger then found an old woman and later her husband, to keep the younger woman company. Then the tiger organized the child birth and a 'prince' was born whose wedding years later, was organized by the tiger again . . . and the legend goes on. This clan therefore worships the tiger, makes offerings to it, and never harms it. Even when the British hunted, they had to omit anyone belonging to the Gond tribe especially the Vagmareuicka clan, from their entourage.

The Gonds live in Mandla district, an area still rich in tigers and where the Kanha National Park provides a refuge for the tiger. The tiger figures prominently in Gond folklore and is always connected to some concept of life and fertility.

One tale explaining the origin of the tiger goes thus: in Kankalpur, Logundi Raja was getting married. His Rani was Hachka Bai. He invited the gods to his wedding. He also called Singbhawani Mata. She thought, 'How am I to travel there?' She took dirt from her two ears and from it made Singh bagh, the greatest of all tigers. Logundi Raja also invited Baba Jalandar. He cut off his penis, which in those days was very long, and turned it into a cobra and hung it round his neck. He gave the old cobra seven sisters—Kariya, Asariya, Jaddu, Dandakarail, Hardariya, Sua, and Sat Bahini. Singbhawani Mata and Baba Jalandar then sat on the two tigers and, followed by the snakes, set out for the wedding.

The tigers turned into horses on the way. When they reached

Logundi Raja's palace, the servant tied them up and gave them grass, but they would not eat it. There was a pig there for the entertainment of the guests. The horses broke their tethering ropes and devoured the pig. Since then, there have been tigers and they have lived on flesh.

Among all the forest communities that worship the tiger, every part of a dead tiger is considered medicinal, much like in Chinese medicine. The whiskers are deemed to have the ability to create a slow and fatal poison much like among South-East Asian forest communities. Among the Gonds, marriages were sanctified after the 'possession' of the ceremony by the Tiger God Bagheshwar, and on certain occasions the possessed man killed a live goat with his teeth.

In Deori, men metamorphosed into tigers and vice versa through the eating of special roots. Were-tigers in this region were recognizable by the absence of a tail. There was widespread belief among forest communities that witches could take the form of tigers, again emphasizing the feminine power of the tiger.

Amongst those who worshipped the tiger, an altar was erected at the spot where a tiger had killed a man. The shrine was in the charge of *Baiga* or a priest who would light lamps and make offerings of cocks or pigs at that spot. Passers-by would throw stones at it. This kept the spirit of the dead at rest and the ghost of the tiger calm, otherwise the spirit of the dead man would walk and the tiger would turn ferocious. The Gonds would build the image of a tiger with mud and stone at the spot where a tiger had killed a man. These images were then propitiated; this offering to the tiger, it was thought, would help in restraining the tiger from future attacks.

Among the Rajputs of Jodhpur there is the story of Rao Siha of Jodhpur and his Rani Chawada who were sleeping in the palace. The Rani dreamt of three tigers that came and took her intestines out of her womb. She told her husband of her dream and he stated that she would now definitely have three sons who would be as strong as tigers.

Pepita Seth, a research scholar on temple rituals in Kerala, relates the story of Ayyappa:

Deep within the thick forests of the Western Ghats nestles a small hill temple whose presiding deity, Ayyappa, the Lord of Sabarimala, is one of Kerala's oldest and most popular Hindu gods. Although there is a certain amount of evidence to suggest that he was a Dravidian tribal hero before he was elevated to a divine status, the cult of the young boy–god is now so enmeshed in legend that it is impossible to disentangle the facts of history from the web of religious myth. In religious terms Ayyappa represents an ideal, a god who may be approached by all men regardless of caste, creed or faith and before whom all men find themselves equal, regardless of their background or status.

Ayyappa's creation is said to have occurred after Vishnu had taken the form of the enchantress Mohini in order to distract the *asuras* when the Cosmic Ocean of Milk was being churned. Mohini was so beautiful that even Shiva was overcome and, for a brief moment, their forms united and Ayyappa was instantly born. The young godling was then left on the banks of the Pampa River in Kerala, to be found by the childless king of Pandalam. Seeing Ayyappa as an answer to his prayers the king took the child back to his queen and together they brought him up as their son. All went well until the queen unexpectedly gave birth to a son and began to favour him more than Ayyappa even though the king declared that the young boy he had found in the forest would be his heir.

Gradually the queen became insanely jealous of Ayyappa and, with the help of the kingdom's Chief Minister, plotted to get rid of him. They decided that she should feign a serious illness and have the royal physician say she could only be cured by drinking tiger's milk—knowing full well that Ayyappa would offer to obtain it for her and be killed.

The plot was successful and as the queen watched Ayyappa set forth on his mission, she was content, certain she would never see him again. However what neither she or the king knew was that the purpose of Ayyappa's creation was to kill the demon Mahishi and that the time had come for him to perform this task. No sooner had he entered the forest than he met Mahishi and, after a great battle, killed her. This is like a mirror image of Durga killing Mahishasura.

Meanwhile the king of Pandalam awaited the return of his adopted son, unaware of his queen's evil scheme and genuinely anxious for the boy's safety. When at last word came that Ayyappa had been sighted, the king rushed to greet him—only to halt in astonishment when he saw that the young boy was riding a great she-tiger, accompanied by her cubs and carrying a vessel containing her milk. Instantly recognising the boy's divinity, the king prostrated before him while his queen, humbled and repentant, begged for forgiveness. The royal couple implored the god to stay with them but he explained that with his mission on earth achieved he must leave although he would always protect their kingdom—and his devotees.

The pilgrimage to Ayyappa's temple is an arduous one, undertaken after a 41-day penance. His devotees—mostly men as women are not allowed to approach Sabarimala's celibate god during their fertile years—have to trek for many miles through thick jungles, walking along rough paths. From the middle of every November thousands and thousands of pilgrims set out for Sabarimala, their pilgrimage recalling Ayyappa's journey into the jungle to collect the tiger's milk, a pilgrimage said to be symbolic of the soul's journey to unite with the Supreme Absolute. When Ayyappa went into the forest he carried with him an *irumudi,* a cloth bag divided into two sections. All Sabarimala pilgrims carry such a bag on their heads. The rear section contains food for the journey, its consumption representing the gradual casting off of worldly needs and desires. The front section holds a coconut filled with ghee—symbolic of the body and the soul—the union with the Absolute occurring when the ghee is poured over the Sabarimala idol and the emptied coconut consumed by flames.[59]

Tiger connections are endless throughout India in a variety of different indigenous cultures. In a way, the tiger was a vital common link between diverse cultures.

This story of the compassionate prince giving his body to save the lives of a starving tigress and her cubs, is told with variations in several Buddhist books. According to one version there was once, many *kalpas* (aeons) before the time of Gautam Buddha, a king of a great country, the name of which is not given. But the name of the king was Maharatna (or Maharatha), and he had three sons, the youngest of whom was called Mahasattva. This prince grew up to be good and gentle and very compassionate to all living creatures. It so happened that one day he and his brothers were strolling over the hills when they saw, near the foot of a precipice, a tigress with two cubs. The tigress was reduced to a skeleton, and was so mad with hunger that she was about to eat her young ones. Seeing this, Prince Mahasattva left his brothers and, desirous of saving the animal's life and the lives of her cubs, threw himself down the precipice and then lay still for the tigress to eat him. But she was too weak and exhausted to even bite. So he pricked himself with a sharp thorn and thus drew blood. By licking this blood the wild beast gained strength and then she devoured the prince, leaving only his bones. When his parents found these, they had them buried and then raised a mound or tope at the grave. This Mahasattva was the Buddha in one of his numerous preparatory stages of existence as a Bodhisattva. It is significant that the story related here did not remain a mere legend in Buddhist texts; the sentiment was wholly endorsed by all and the spot where the event was supposed to have taken place was revered and commemorated by a *stupa*.*

It is again a mixture of awe for the power of the tiger and the symbolic magic with which it is invested, that determines the relationship between man and tiger in many parts of tribal India. The concomitant values of power and fear led to the tiger being worshipped. Added to these was the belief in the tiger as an agent of fertility and this was of prime importance in societies where the produce of the earth and the labour of men and women determined survival in an almost one-to-one equation. The association of the tiger with fertility is most clearly evident in tribal myths.

In one story, a man and woman were in the jungle. There were no others. Asur Dano stopped them copulating. Many days passed and the woman thought in her mind, 'What shall we do? This Asur has stopped all the joy of our life.' She cut a branch from an ebony tree and cut off a lot of little bits. She threw them at the Asur and they turned into bears and chased him. She threw shavings of the saleh tree at him and they turned into tigers. She said to them, 'Go and guard our camp. Do not let the Asur near us.' The bears, hyenas, and tigers prowled

*It is 7000 ft. high in the mountains of Nepal and is called Namobuddha.

round and round keeping the Asur far away. The man and woman copulated and there was seed and fruit.

Bagheshwar, the Tiger God, is present in different manifestations among a variety of people in India, particularly among the Vindhyan and other hill tribes. The tigress, too, is worshipped as Baghir Devi. Among some tribes the worship is extensive enough to include priests who claim knowledge of tiger lore and who tend Bagh deo shrines, built at spots where a tiger has killed a man. Such priests claim immunity from death by a tiger and the more daring extend this immunity to the villagers as well. It is said that such priests have the power to bewitch tigers.

One story about how they acquired such immunity goes thus:

In Dhutiadongri lived a Baiga whose name was Latia. His wife was pregnant. One day the Baiga and his wife went to the jungle to dig roots. The Baiga dug in one place, his wife in another. As she was digging, the Baigan's pains began and she shouted to her husband. 'O Dewar, my belly is hurting me!' As she said this a God came upon the Baiga and he cried, 'Ochha, Ochha!' and presently he said to his wife, 'O Dewarin, if a boy is born do not bring it to me but only bring it if it is a girl.' As the poor woman was weeping in her pain she called out to the Baiga, 'But why should I not if the child is a boy?' The Baiga answered, 'If it is a boy, I will have to go to someone else's house to get him a bride and I will have to touch another's feet but if it is a girl people will come to my house and they will fall at my feet.' As they were talking, a child was born and it was a boy. When the Baiga saw it he grew red with anger and with his digging stick he knocked off some chips from a saja tree and holding them in his hand uttered a spell and turned the chips into a tiger and tigress that should devour the child. When the mother saw them, she left the child on the ground and ran away. But when the tiger and tigress found the child, they said to each other, 'What is the use of such a little creature? We cannot fill our bellies with this,' and they took the boy home and cared for him. When the boy grew up, he looked after the tiger and tigress who had grown very thin because of scarcity of food. He used to hunt for them with his bow and arrow and cared for them in every way until they died. This is why the tiger and the Baiga are friends. The tiger was created by the Baiga and the Baiga boy was brought up and cared for by the tiger.

Probably the most widespread sanctity that the tiger has in India is as Durga's vehicle. As such, the tiger is revered not just by various forest and tribal communities but in the 'greater' Hindu tradition. The image of the tiger as sacred vehicle has parallels in Siberia's winged tiger spirit, China's Taoist popes vehicles, and Tibet's goddess who rides tigers as depicted in frescoes.

Durga was the supreme goddess who could bring light on earth, peace after conquering the forces of evil. The energy of the gods to fight evil took on the form of Durga. They in fact created a feminine force or *shakti* to combat the evil male power on earth. From Durga sprang the goddess Kali to join the fierce battle against evil. Durga means 'beyond reach' and her vehicle in her fight was the tiger. The tiger represented shakti, was a repository of feminine force being born of the Earth Mother, and was unmatched on earth as an animal form. Both Durga and the tiger derived their strength from the Earth Mother and together were the most powerful repository of power against evil. In many ways, they were joined together in battle and without each other, the battle might have been lost.

When the British colonized India, it was full of rich forests and an array of birds and animals, among them innumerable tigers. In one of these areas in lower Bengal where vast tracts are covered with mangrove swamps that sweep into Bangladesh, the tiger still has its largest population on the subcontinent, probably 300–400, on both sides of the border. The tiger was propitiated like a god here. In north Bengal the Tiger God was called Sonarai, in east Bengal, Barekhan Gazi, and was worshipped by both Hindus and Muslims. Scroll paintings depicted the *gazi* or holy man of the Muslims carrying a string of prayer beads and a staff, astride a tiger and attacking all that was evil. Among the Santals of Bihar too the Tiger God is very important as is the invocation of the tiger spirit.

L. De Grandpre, a French traveller in the early eighteenth century writes of Bengal's mangrove swamps and their abundance of tigers:

This point forms the southern extremity of the woods of sondry, famous for the enormous size of the tigers which are found there, and with which they are filled.

Some of them are as large as oxen. Their coat is variegated with stripes of reddish yellow and black, and is whitish under the belly. They are so eager and ferocious in pursuit of their prey, that they have been known to throw themselves into the water, and swim to attack boats on the river.

Notwithstanding the superiority which these creatures possess over human beings by their strength, ferocity and the arms with which nature has supplied them, a certain instinct seems to tell them, that men by their intellectual faculties are still more formidable than they; hence they avoid inhabited and cultivated places; or if they sometimes visit them, it is only when compelled by hunger.

But between this place and the Clive islands they are so numerous, that they are sometimes seen in troops on the banks. These islands have been lately brought into a state of improvement for the cultivation of sugar. The clearing of the ground was attended with the loss of a great number of Indians, who were destroyed by these ferocious animals; for, in cutting down the wood with which the face of the country was covered, they were disturbed in their retreats, and rushed upon the labourers. What will appear extraordinary, these men never attempted to defend themselves, though their number sometimes amounted to five hundred.[60]

Small wonder that 'these men' couldn't defend themselves against a creature they regarded as God who could hardly be denied the right to protect his home.

Louis Rosselet towards the end of the last century describes British efforts to cultivate the Sunderbans:

Since the English have tried to develop the cultivation of rice in the Sunderbunds, they have furnished the natives with strychnine, and several tigers have perished by the poison. Their numbers, however, have as yet been scarcely reduced, for during the night we heard a concert of hoarse roars round us on all sides.

We had visible proofs that parts of the Sunderbunds were even at the present day on the high road to prosperity; and some islands whereon English men have established themselves exhibited magnificent cultivation of rice, fine indigo and sugar plantations.[61]

The traditional pattern of life of man, tiger, and forest that had coexisted peacefully for centuries was on the brink of being uprooted. A hundred years of British rule took an immense toll on India's forests and fauna and consequently on the basic fibre of its beliefs that were so intimately bound up with nature. Meanwhile the British left endless accounts of encounters with tigers in their senseless and wanton trophy hunting. Colonel Pollack narrates in *Incidents of Foreign Sport and Travel,* published in 1894,

I do not think I could have borne the gruesome sight much longer, when there was a roar, and a brindled mass sprang at something which was invisible to me. Instantaneously a vast speckled body coiled itself round the brindled matter, there was a struggle, bones seemed to be crunched to bits, the tiger gave a feeble roar or two, and then all was still except an occasional convulsive up heaving.[62]

Colonel Pollack was atop a tree on a *machan* waiting to shoot a man-eating tiger near the corpse of a victim.

That long, long night at length terminated, and thankful I was to see the dawn of day and hear the jungle fowls proclaim that sunrise was at hand. Losing no time I descended to solve last night's mystery, the sight that met my eyes was marvellous. A huge rock snake, a python, just over twenty-one feet in length, lay coiled round the body of the tiger whose fangs in turn were imbedded in the back of the snake's head, while the reptile's folds, after enveloping the tiger, 'had got' a purchase by lashing its tail round the adjoining sapling, and so assisted, the vast muscular power it possessed in crushing the tiger to death.

Having procured coolies, with the united strength of twenty men, aided with coils of strong rope, we unwound the snake from its hold on the tree, when a cart being procured, the two, lying dead in each other's embrace, were conveyed to the village.[63]

This remarkable incident, according to the author, occurred in the Wynaud Forests near Coimbatore.

After the British left, Indian politicians and princes accentuated a process of deforestation and exploitation that has left India's forests in a very precarious state. Besides, with tiger hunting having been established as a powerful symbol of manhood, the tiger was facing a powerful threat of extinction. In a way over the last centuries, the killing of a tiger for those who ruled and were powerful, was a symbol of manhood; an array of important people roamed India's forests to prove themselves. I have personally been through the records of at least 20,000 tigers shot between 1860 and 1960.

Forest communities were undergoing rapid changes as 'modern policy measures' were imposed on their lives. Development in post-independent India has been piece-meal and generally short-term oriented and blind to the future. This meant that by 1970 the tigers of India were a lost species. Finally a ban on their hunting was enforced but only after an estimated tiger population of 40,000–50,000 at the beginning of the twentieth century had dwindled to a mere 1800.

Conclusion

In our journey through the tiger's forests, extending from Siberia to Indonesia and branching off into Burma and India, we have encountered a rich and diverse fund of tiger folklore, belief, and ritual (although only the tip of the iceberg has been touched in these pages). We have seen images of princesses riding tigers' backs, tigers turning white after 500 years and then attaining immortality after another 500 as stars in the milky way, and from there continuing to exercise a beneficial influence on earth, were-tigers, tigers tending humans, tigers protecting forests, tigers as the feminine Chinese force 'yin', and tigers as destroyers of evil as Durga's vehicle. We have heard of the magical and potent curative powers of each part of the tiger's body. But above all we have seen that whatever the particular form, the tiger was worshipped everywhere throughout its domain. Before the advent of the European with his gun, his search for manhood-affirming trophies, and his irrational fear of the tiger, the tiger was indeed the king of his jungles. Man and tiger lived in complete harmony and although tiger-killing often formed an important part of the ceremonial of forest communities, elaborate taboos surrounded its killing for any purpose other than the ceremonial.

In most post-colonial polities of Asia, particularly those of India, conservation policies squarely lay the blame for tiger-killing on poaching by forest communities, and work towards their exclusion from protected areas. Perhaps, to a certain extent, these may be the culprit, but it must be remembered that this is only after the march of civilization has almost completely destroyed the tiger's traditional ways of life. If the vastly depleted tiger population is to have any future at all, it appears that attempts must be made to salvage whatever is left of the tradition linking man with tiger, and for working towards inclusivist rather than exclusivist policies regarding forest communities.

End Notes

1. T.N. Atkinson, *Travels in the Regions of the Upper and Lower Amur*, New York, 1860.

2. J.G. Frazer, *Worship of Nature*, London, 1926.

3. U.K. Arseniev, *Dersu the Trapper*, London, 1939.

4. Ibid.

5. C.S. Cumberland, *Sport on the Pamirs and Turkestan Steppes*, London, 1875.

6. D. Carruthers, *Beyond the Caspian*, London, 1949.

7. Ibid.

8. A.E. Cavendish, *Korea and the Sacred White Mountain*, London, 1894.

9. Ibid.

10. S. Bergman, *In Korean Wilds and Villages*, 1922.

11. A.E. Cavendish, *Korea and the Sacred White Mountain*, London, 1894.

12. A. Hosie, *Manchuria—Its People, Resources and Recent History*, London, 1910.

13. A. Adams, *Travels of a Naturalist in Japan and Manchuria*, London, 1870.

14. P. Yelts, *The Symbolism in Chinese Art*, China Society, 1912.

15. B. Karlgren, *Some Fecundity Symbols in Ancient China* (No Date).

16. M. Lipton, *The Tiger Rugs of Tibet*, London, 1988.

17. *Chinese Materia Medica*, 1597, Published 1931 in Peking Natural History Bulletin.

18. Ibid.

19. Ibid.

20. H.R. Davies, *Travels in China*, 1896.

21. R.C. Andrews, *Camps and Travels in China*, London, 1919.

22. Ibid.

23. H.R. Caldwell, *Blue Tiger*, London, 1925.

24. Ibid.

25. L. Houji, Personal Communication.

26. G.A.C. Herklots, *South China Morning Post*, 1951.

27. W. Baze, *Tiger Tiger*, London, 1957.

28. P. Alexander, *Spirits of the Malay Jungles*, Asia, January 1935.

29. Ibid.

30. W. Baze, *Tiger Tiger*, London, 1957.

31. Ibid.

32. M.H. Bradley, *Trailing the Tiger*, London, 1929.

33. Ibid.

34. W. Baze, *Tiger Tiger*, London, 1957.

35. Ibid.

36. H. Monhot, *Travels in Indo-China*, 1864.

37. Ibid.

38. A. Locke, *The Tigers of Trengganu*, London, 1907.

39. G. Maxwell, *In Malay Forests*, London, 1907.

40. A. Locke, *The Tigers of Trengganu*, London, 1954.

41. Ibid.

42. C. Collingwood, *Rambles of a Naturalist*, London, 1869.

43. Ibid.

44. J. Bradley, *A Narrative of Travel and Sport in Burma, Siam and the Malay Peninsula*, London, 1876.

45. A.H. Everett, *Journal of the Straits*, 1880.

46. Ibid.

47. T. Schilling, *Tigermen of Anai*, London, 1952.

48. Ibid.

49. Ibid.

50. H. Monhot, *Travels in Indo-China*, 1864.

51. T. Schilling, *Tigermen of Anai*, London, 1952.

52. Ibid.

53. Ibid.

54. A. Vambery, *Travels in Central Asia*, London, 1864.

55. J.H. Hutton, *The Angami Nagas*, London, 1921.

56. P. Jayakar, *The Earthen Drum*, New Delhi, 1981, and Personal Communication.

57. Ibid.

58. Y. Dalmia, *The Painted World of the Warlis*, Delhi, 1988.

59. P. Seth, Personal Communication.

60. L.D. Grandpre, *Sundarbunds* (No Date).

61. L. Rosselet, *India and its Native Princes*, 1882.

62. T. Pollack, *Incidents of Foreign Sport and Travel*, London, 1894.

63. Ibid.

Afterword

I firmly believe that true conservation values exist in a nation because of the religions, rituals, myths, and legends that abound in the traditions of the people. India's religions focused on the respect for nature—many rituals integrated wild animals and trees with a core of belief. Therefore even before the word 'conservation' was defined, it already existed in the very fabric of the people—and thus the cult around the tiger which goes back thousands of years.

What on earth would have happened to the tiger without the cult that enveloped it? I am completely convinced that without the belief and ritual that engulfed the land of the tiger we would have no tigers left today. I think that enormous damage was done to the tiger in the last fifty years by continuous changes in the cultural fabric of people across Asia—this process accelerated rapidly in the last fifteen years as changing economic models dotted the landscape of Asia.

In many ways tiger conservation strategies that had their origins in the 1970s helped to minimize some of the damage that had percolated

across the land of the tiger. And the impact of these strategies was successful because millions of forest dwellers believed in the power of the tiger, preferring to fear and respect it rather than kill it. Of course, because of the economic models and greed for quick money, many mafias evolved to poach tigers and fuel the market for tiger bones and skins. But I believe strongly that the majority of forest dwellers across Asia still refrained from any direct harm to the tiger.

The last fifteen years have seen an enormous growth in the electronic media, and television has entangled human life, especially in urban areas. Its most negative effect has been on the cultural fabric of the people. A younger generation has popped up across Asia that chooses to negate traditional values, and for the first time, a sharp decline has occurred in tiger beliefs. In my opinion this is the primary reason for the decline in the world's tiger population. It is also the reason why tiger conservation strategies have less impact than they had before. In my travels across South Asia, I have discovered right across forest villages a great sympathy for both tiger and forest amongst village elders, but the younger generation has no care or concern. The little control over them comes only from the elders, otherwise we would have seen some of the worst kind of exploitation of the land of the tiger. In over-populated regions of Asia, television and with it the consumption of the so-called 'goodies' of life that are advertised on the box, have reached alarming proportions. And because these regions are so desperately poor, money can only be made by devastating forests, wildlife and the wilderness. And this takes on a menacing shape when cultural beliefs fade, especially since greed has become overpowering and corruption rampant. This is what is happening. The cult of the tiger is slowly fading away and as we engage in the final battle to save this superb animal, we are losing key supporters across the wilderness. Twenty-five years ago few would have ventured from their village to kill tigers but today more and more are willing to take that risk, fuelled by the so-called 'promises' of a new life that the media has so intensely projected.

An analysis of the electronic media reveals that its most potent impact has been 'to brainwash' its audience and to addict it to the 'non-sense' of the screen. God save the tiger. India in the twenty-first century has over one billion people and also boasts of half the world's tiger population, half the world's Asiatic elephant population and along with these charismatic species, an array of other living organisms. Could any of this have been possible without a core belief in nature? Could the Asiatic elephant have been safe without a belief in Ganesha, the Elephant God? Could the tiger have survived had it not been the vehicle of Durga? And would the snake, the turtle, the peacock, the cranes and some of our trees survived without a bank of beliefs in them?

It is the cult around an animal, around nature itself that forms such a deep part of so many religions like Hinduism, Buddhism and Jainism. It is these beliefs of people that keep some vital components of our wilderness alive—let us never forget the Bishnoi people of the great desert regions in India—their belief in complete non-violence towards living organisms has resulted in the survival of desert wildlife, be it black buck or chinkara. Without them and their incredible courage and sacrifice, little would have been left.

Let us never forget that the last fifteen years have seen the weakest forms of governance in the sectors of forest and wildlife. Political leadership has failed the wilderness, our laws have been endlessly violated, and the administration of this sector has had the lowest priority ever. As levels of violence across Asia have increased, so have forest and wildlife crimes. A complete lack of law enforcement and the conviction of the guilty have led many to believe 'that you can get away with murdering nature'. Yet against all odds some of the most endangered species of this country survived the pressures. We still have 2000–2500 tigers, 25,000 elephants and in surviving fragments of forest, a diversity of other species.

The reason comes from a fear and respect of nature. It is the cultural belief system of our people that delayed the extinction of many species, and the sheer impact of this countered the excessively exploitative forces of the last two decades.

Now what? The cultural beliefs have been smashed and this pounding continues. I fear the worst. A new generation with little attention to past traditions has grown across Asia—this has already impacted on the wilderness of Asia that slowly fragments and fades away. The cult of the tiger in the twenty-first century also slips away. With it the wild tigers of Asia disappear. Maybe if we are lucky, a handful of National Parks across Asia will survive and be tiny examples of what the land of the tiger once was . . . and this only if we are able to make some of the strictest protection strategies for our wilderness. As the cult of the tiger fades we need to fill the gap being created by new and innovative protection measures—if these do not come into place, then exploitative policies fuelled by greed will envelop our wilderness—it has only been countered so far by the belief system. As the belief system dies, the forces of exploitation turn into a monster, and to stop it requires new policy and intervention that protects the little that is left. We must rapidly act before it is too late—reform and restructuring the mechanisms of governance become the top-most priority. We can no longer lean on the amazing and powerful cult of the tiger to save it.

Select Bibliography

USSR

Abramov, V.K. *A contribution to the biology of the Amur tiger* panthera tigris longipilis *(Fitzinger, 1868) Vestnik Ceskoslovenske Spolecnosti Zoologicke* 26(2):189–202.

Aramliev, I. *Beyond the Ural Mountains*, London 1961.

Atkinson, T.N. *Oriental and Western Siberia*, 1858.

———. *Travels in the Regions of the Upper and Lower Amur*, New York 1860.

Coxwell, C. Fillingham (comp./ed.) *Siberian and Other Folk Tales,* London 1925.

Dyrenkova, N.P. 'Bear worship among Turkish Tribes of Siberia', in *Proceedings of the Twenty-Third International Congress of Americanists*, 1928 (pp. 411–40) New York 1930.

Knystantas, A. *The Natural History of the USSR*, Century Hutchison, London 1987.

Matjushkin, E.N., Smirnov, E.N. and Zhyvotchenko, V.I. *The Amur Tiger in the USSR.*

Mazak, V. *Notes on Siberian long-haired tiger,* Panthera tigris altaica *(Temminck,*

1844), with a remark on Temminck's mammal volume of the Fauna Japonica Mammalia 31(4):537–73.

Novikov, G. *Carnivorous Mammals of the Fauna of the USSR*, IPST, Washington DC 1962.

Ognev, S. *Mammals of the USSR and Adjacent Countries, III*, IPST, Washington DC 1962.

Prynn, D. *Siberian Tiger Wildlife* 20(9):398–402, 1978.

Rostovtzev, Michael I. *The Animal Style in Southern Russia and China*, Princeton 1929.

Smirnov, E.N. *The Tiger in the USSR*, IUCN, 1977.

Stroganov, S.U. *Carnivorous Mammals of Siberia*, IUCN, 1969.

Swayne, H.O.C. *Through the Highland of Siberia*, London 1964.

CHINA

Allen, G.M. *Mammals of China and Mongolia*, American Museum of Natural History, New York 1938.

Andrews, R.C. *Camps and Travels in China*, London 1919.

_____. *Ends of the Earth* London, 1929.

Baikov, N.A. *The Manchurian Tiger*, London 1925.

Caldwell, H. Ruth *Blue Tiger*, London 1925.

Chen-Huang, Shou *Economic Animals of China*, Peiping 1962.

Church, P.W. *Chinese Turkestan with Caravan and Rifle*, London 1901.

Clarke, Samuel R. *Among the Tribes in South-West China*, 1970.

Colbert, E.H. and Hooijer, D.H. *Pleistocene Mammals from the Limestone Fissures of Szechwan*, China Bulletin of the American Museum of Natural History 102(1):1–134, 1935.

Eberhard, Wolfram *Studies in Chinese Folklore and Related Essays*, Indiana University Press, Bloomington 1970.

Granet, Marcel *Danses et Légendes de la Chine ancienne*, 2 vols, Paris 1926.

_____. *La pensée chinoise*, Paris 1934.

Hooijer, D.A. *Pleistocene Remains of* Panthera tigris *(Linnaeus) subspecies from Wanhsien, Szechan, China, compared with fossil and recent tigers from other localities*, American Museum Novitiates No. 1346, p. 17, 1947.

Lanning, G. *Wildlife in China*, London 1911.

Lattimore, O. *Desert Road to Turkestan*, London 1928.

———. *High Tartary*, Boston 1930.

———. *Inner Asian Frontiers of China*, New York 1940.

Pei, Wen-Chung *On the Carnivora from locality 1 of Choukoutien*, Palaeontologica Sinica, Series C, 8(1):1–216, 1934.

Prejvalski, N.M. *Mongolia, the Tangut Country*, London 1876.

Quincy, J.W. *Chinese Hunter*, London 1939.

Rock, Joseph *The Ancient Nakhi Kingdom of South-East China*, Harvard University Press, 1947.

Sowerby, A. de C. *The Naturalist in Manchuria*, London 1928.

———. *A Naturalist's Notebook in China*, London 1925.

———. *Sport and Science on the Sino-Mongolian Frontier*, London 1918.

———. *Fur and Feather in North China*, Tsientsin 1914.

Sutton, J.B. *In China's Border Provinces; the turbulent career of Joseph Rock— botanist/explorer*, Hastings Home.

Swinhoe, R. 'On the mammals of the island of Formosa (China) in *Proceedings of the Zoological Society*, London 1862: 347–65.

———. 'On the mammals of Hainan' in *Proceedings of the Zoological Society*, London 1870:224–39.

Wallace, H.F. *Big game of Central and Western China*, London 1913.

Werner, Chalmers *A Dictionary of Chinese Mythology*, Kelly & Walsh, Shanghai 1932.

Williams, C.A.S. *Outlines of Chinese Symbolism and Art Motives*, Customs College Press, Peking 1931.

Yelts, Perceval *The Symbolism in Chinese Art*, China Society 1912.

MALAYA, INDO-CHINA AND INDONESIA

Alexander, Patrick *Spirits of the Malay Jungles*, Asia, January 1935, Vol. XXXV No. 1.

Borner, M. *Status and conservation of the Sumatran Tiger*, Carnivore 1(1):97–102, 1978.

Bradley, J. *A Narrative of Travel and Sport in Burma, Siam and the Malay Peninsula*, London 1876.

Cole, Fay-Cooper *The Peoples of Malaysia*, New York 1945.

Durand, M. *Imagerie Populaire Vietnamienne*, EFEO.

Evans, Ivor H.N. *Studies in Religion, Folklore and Custom in British North Borneo and the Malay Peninsula*, Cambridge University Press, 1923.

Foenander, E.C. *Big Game of Malaya*, London 1952.

Harrison, A. *Indo-China: a Sportsman's Opportunity*, Plymouth 1937.

Hemmer, H. 'Fossil mammals of Java II: Zur Fossilgeschichte des Tigers (*Panthera tigris* [L])' in *Java Proccedings of the Koninklijke Nederlandse Akademie van Wetenschappen*, Series B, 74(1):35–52, 1971.

Hubback, T.R. *Studies of Wildlife in a Malayan Jungle*, Bombay Natural History Society.

———. *Three months after Big Game in Pahang*, Bombay Natural History Society.

Kitchener, H.J. *Malayan Nature Journal* 1961.

Maxwell, G. *In Malay Forests*, Blackwood, London 1907.

Mazak, V. *On the Bali Tiger*, Panthera tigris balica (Schwarz 1912), *Vestnik Ceskoslovenske Spolecnosti Zoologicke* 40(3):179–95, 1967.

Mazak, V., Groves, C.P. and Van Bree, P.J.H. 'On a skin and skull of the Bali tiger and a list of preserved specimens of *Panthera tigris balica* (Schwarz, 1912)' in *Zeitschrift für Saugetierkunde* 43(2):65–128, 1978.

Medway, Lord *The Wild Animals of Malaya*, OUP, London 1969.

Meyer, C. *Trapping Wild Animals in Malayan Jungles*, London 1922.

Monestrol, H. De *Hunting Wild Animals of Indo-China*, Saigon 1952.

Monhot, H. *Travels in Indo-China*, 1864.

Peacock, E.H. *A Game Book for Burma and Adjoining Territories*, London.

Skeat, W.W. *Malay Magic*, 1900.

———. *Pagan Races of the Malay Peninsula*, 1906.

Stuart-Fox, D.T. *Macan: The Balinese Tiger*, Bali Post (Eng. edn.), 23 July 1979 pp. 12–13.

Wessing, Robert *The Soul of Ambiguity: the tiger in South-East Asia*, Centre for South-East Asian Studies, Northern Illinois University.

NEPAL, BURMA AND TIBET

Berglie, Per-Arne *On the Question of Tibetan Shamanism*, Zurich 1978.

Corneille, Jest *Tarap; one himalayan Valley*, 1974.

Gray, James *Burmese Proverbs and Maxims*.

Gribble, R.H. *Out of the Burma Night*, London 1943.

Hitchkock, J. and Jones, R. *Spirit Possession in the Nepal Himalayas*, Warminster 1975.

Kinloch, A.A. *Large Game Shooting in Tibet and the North-West*, London 1876.

Lipton, Mimi *The Tiger Rugs of Tibet* Hayward Gallery, London 1988.

Morris, J. *Winter in Nepal*, London 1963.

Roerich, J.N. *The Animal Style among the Nomad Tribes of Northern Tibet*, Seminarium Kondakovianum, Prague 1930.

Smythies, E.A. *Big Game Shooting in Nepal*, Thacker, Spink & Co., Calcutta.

Stainton, J.D.A. *Forest of Nepal* Murray, London 1972.

INDIA

Baldwin, J. *The Large and Small Game of Bengal and the North-Western Provinces of India*, London 1877.

Bannerjee, S.C. *Flora and Fauna in Sanskrit Literature*, Calcutta 1932.

Berriedale-Keith, A. *Indian Mythology*, Boston 1917.

Chandra, Subodh and Mode, Heinz *Indian Folk Art*.

Crooke, William *Religion and Folklore of Northern India*, OUP, London 1926.

Dalmia, Y. *The Painted World of the Warlis*, Lalit Kala Academy 1988.

Dalton, E.T. *Descriptive Ethnology of Bengal*, Calcutta 1872.

Dowson, J. *A Classical Dictionary of Hindu Mythology*, Trubner's Oriental Series, London 1879.

Dutt, G.S. *The Tiger God in Bengal Art*, Modern Review, Calcutta, November 1932.

Elwin, V. *The Baiga*, London 1939.

———. *The Muria and their Ghotul*, Bombay 1947.

———. *The Tribal Art of Middle India*, London.

Enthoven *The Folklore of Bombay*, Asian Education Service.

Faunthorpe. J.C. *Jungle Life in India, Burma and Nepal*, Natural History No. 2, 1924.

Fernandez, W., Menon, G. and Viegas, P. *Forests, Environment and Tribal Economy (Orissa)*, Indian Social Institute.

Fife-Cookson, Col. J.C. *Tiger shooting in the Doon and Ulwar*, London 1887.

Forbes *Wanderings of a Naturalist*.

Forsyth *Highlands of Central India*.

Gahlot *The Wisdom of Rajputana*.

Grierson, G.A. *Bihar Peasant Life*, Patna.

Gupta, A. 'Tigers at High Altitudes' in *Journal of the Bombay Natural History Society* 29(1–2):55–56, 1959.

Hewett, J. *Jungle Trails in Northern India*, London 1938.

Hiralal, R.B. and Russell, R.V. *The Tribes and Castes of the Central Provinces of India*, London 1916.

Hutton, J.H. *The Angami Nagas*, London 1921.

Inverarity, J. 'Unscientific notes on the tiger' in *Journal of the Bombay Natural History Society* 3(3):143–54, 1888.

Juliusson, Per *The Gonds and their Religion*, Stockholm 1974.

Kanhaiyalal, Sahal *Rajasthani Kahavat Kos*.

Kinloch, A. *Large Game Shooting in Thibet, the Himalayas, Northern and Central India*, Calcutta 1892.

Kosambi, D.D. 'The Culture and Civilization of Ancient India' in *Historical Outline*, No. 104, p. 89, London 1965.

Lewis, E. 'The "sambar call" of the tiger and its explanation' in the *Journal of the Bombay Natural History Society* 41(4):889–90, 1940.

Lydekker, R. *The Game Animals of India, Burma, Malaya and Tibet*, London 1924.

Maury, Curt *Folk Origins of Indian Art*, Columbia University Press, New York 1969.

Milis, J.P. *The Lotha Nagas*, London 1921.

———. *The Ao Nagas*, London 1922.

———. *The Rengma Nagas*, London 1937.

O'Brien, E. 'Where man-eating tigers occur' in *Journal of the Bombay Natural History Society* 45(1):231–2, 1944.

O'Flaherty, W.D. *Sexual Metaphors and Animal Symbols in Indian Mythology*, New Delhi 1980.

Pilgrim, Guy E. *Fossil Carnivora of India*, Calcutta 1932.

Pocock, R. 'Tigers' in *Journal of the Bombay Natural History Society* 33(3):505–41, 1929.

Risley, H.H. *The Tribes and Castes of Bengal*, Calcutta 1891–2.

Rivers, W.H.R. *The Todas*, Macmillan, London 1906.

Roberts, T.J. *The Mammals of Pakistan*, Benn, London 1977.

Rowney, H.B. *The Wild Tribes of India*, London 1882.

Roy, Sarat Chandra *The Birhors: a little-known jungle tribe of Chota Nagpur*, Ranchi, 1925.

———. *The Hill Bhuiyas of Orissa*, Ranchi, Man in India Office 1935.

Sharma, Ram Dutt *Sanskrit Karyon mein pasu paksi*, Jaipur.

Sleeman *Rambles and Recollections*.

Smith, W.C. *The Ao Naga Tribe of Assam*, Macmillan, London.

Stockley, C.H. *Stalking in the Himalayas & Northern India*, 1936.

Stutley, Margaret and James *A Dictionary of Hinduism: its mythology, folklore and development*, Routledge & Kegan Paul, London 1977.

Thurston, E. *Castes and Tribes of Southern India*, Madras 1909.

Trumbull *Blood Covenant*.

Tylor *Primitive Culture*.

Washburn, H.E. *Epic Mythology*, Delhi 1974.

FURTHER READING

Adams, Arthur *Travels of a Naturalist in Japan and Manchuria*, London 1870.

Almeida, W.B. *Life in Java with sketches of the Javanese*, London, Hurst and Blackett (2 volumes), 1864.

Arseniev, U.K. *Dersu the Trapper*, London 1939.

Bakels, J. 'But His Stripes Remain—On the Symbolism of the Tiger in the Oral Tradition of Kerinci, Sumatra' in J.G. Oosten (ed.) *Text and Tales. Studies in the oral tradition*, CNWS Publications 22, Leiden, University of Leiden, 1994.

Baker, L. 'The Siberian Tiger and the Country of Tiger Tales', *Education About Asia* 3/3 pp. 11–16, 1998.

Ball, Katherine *Decorative Motives of Oriental Art* Bodley Head, London 1927.

Banner, H.S. *Romantic Java as it was...*, Seeley, 1927.

Bastin, J. (ed.) *The British in West Sumatra* (1685–1825)—*A selection of documents*, Kuala Lampur, University of Malaya Press, 1965.

Berg, B. *Tiger und Mensch*, Berlin 1934.

———. *Jungle*, Berlin 1935.

Bickmore, A.S. *Travels in the East Indian Archipelago*, London, Murray, 1868.

Bohlin, B. 'The sabre-toothed tigers once more' in *Bulletin of the Geological Institute of Uppsala* 32:11–20, 1947.

Boomgaard, P. 'Death to the Tiger! The Development of Tiger and Leopard Rituals in Java 1605–1906' in *South-East Asia Research*, 2 pp. 141–175, 1994.

———. *Frontiers of Fear—Tigers and People in the Malay World 1600–1950*, Yale University Press, 2001.

Boyes, J. *Tiger-Men and Tofu Dolls—Tribal Spirits in Northern Thailand*, Chiangmai-Silkworm, 1997.

Brittlebank, K. 'Sakti and Barakat: The Power of Tipu's Tiger—An Examination of the Tiger Emblem of Tipu Sultan of Mysore' in *Modern Asian Studies* 29/2 pp. 257–69, 1995.

Carruthers, D. *Unknown Mongolia*, London 1913.

_____. *Beyond the Caspian*, London 1949.

Casserly, G. *In the Green Jungle*, London 1927.

_____. *Dwellers in the Jungle*, London 1925.

Cavendish, A.E.T. *Korea and the Sacred White Mountain*, London 1894.

Clarke, Kenneth *Animals and Men* Thames & Hudson, London 1977.

Collingwood, C. *Rambles of a Naturalist*, 1869.

Cumberland, C.S. *Sport on the Pamirs and Turkestan Steppes*, London 1875.

Dasgupta, S.B. *Obscure Religious Cults*, Calcutta 1976.

Digby, G. *Tigers, Gold and Witchdoctors*, London 1928.

Endicott, K.M. *An Analysis of Malay Magic*, Oxford, Clarendon, 1970.

Evans, I.H.N. *The Negritos of Malaya*, Cambridge, Cambridge University Press, 1937.

Fisher, J. 'Tiger! Tiger!' in *International Wildlife* 8(3)4–11 1978.

Forbes, H.O. *A Naturalist's Wanderings in the Eastern Archipelago*, New York, Harper, 1885.

Frazer, J. *The Golden Bough*, No. 113, p. 519, Toronto 1965.

Frazer, J.G. *Worship of Nature*, London 1926.

Gimlette, J.Q. *Many Poisons and Charm Cures*, London, Churchill, 1915, 1923.

Harington, C.R. 'Pleistocene remains of the lion-like cat (*Panthera atrox*) from the Yukon Territory and Northern Alaska' in *Canadian Journal of Earth Sciences* 6:1277–88, 1969.

Harrington Jr., Fred A. *A Guide to the Mammals of Iran*, Tehran 1972.

Harrison, David L. *Mammals of Arabia* Benn, London 1968.

Hastings, J. ed. *Encyclopedia of Religion and Ethics* IV & V, Edinburgh 1964, No. 26, p. 8.

Knowles, G.H. *Terrors of the Jungle*, London 1932.

Koch-Isenburg, L. *Through the Jungle Very Softly*, London 1963.

Lammens, H. *Islam: Beliefs and Institutions*, Methuen 1929.

Leslie, Charles ed. *Anthropology of Folk Religion*, Vintage Books, New York 1960.

Lindgren, E.J. 'The Reindeer Tungus of Manchuria' in *Journal of the Royal Central Asian Society*, London XXII, April 1935, pp. 221–31.

Long, Rev. J. *Eastern Proverbs and Emblems*, Trubner's Oriental Series, London.

Malet, R. *When the Red Gods Call*, London 1934.

———. *Unforgiving Minutes*, London 1934.

Mcneely, Jeffrey A. and Wachtel, Paul S. *The Soul of the Tiger*, Doubleday, 1988.

Mitchell, K.W.S. *Tales from Some Eastern Jungles*, London 1928.

Neff, Nancy, A. *The Big Cats*, Abrams, New York 1986.

Nyuak, Leo 'Religious Rites and Customs of the Iban or Dyaks of Sarawak' in *Anthropos*, I pp. 11–23, 165–84, 403–25, 1906.

Sutton, R.L. *Tiger Trails in Southern Asia*, London 1926.

Tate, G.H.H. *Mammals of Eastern Asia*, London 1947.

Tilson, Ronald L. and Seal, Ulysses S. (eds) *Tigers of the World*, New York 1987.

———. *Tiger—an Endangered Species*, Noyers, New Jersey.

Toynbee, Jocelyn *Animals in Roman Life and Art*, Thames & Hudson, London 1976.

Turnbull, Colin *The Forest People*.

Vambery, A. *Travels in Central Asia*, Murray, London 1864.

Volker, T. *The Animal in Far Eastern Art*, E.J. Brill, Leiden 1975.

Voorhoeve, R. *Harimau*, London 1957.

Wallihan, A.G. *Camera Shots at Big Game*, 1901.

Wensinck, A.J. *Tree and Bird as Cosmological Symbols in Western Asia*, Amsterdam 1921.

Wessing, R. *The Soul of Ambiguity—The Tiger in Southeast Asia* (monograph), Northern Illinois University, 1986.

Widengren, George *The King and the Tree of Life in Ancient Near Eastern Religion*, Uppsala 1951.

Wood, H. *The Shores of Lake Aral*, London 1876.

Yi Sang, O. *Wild Animals of Korea*, Saigon.

Zozayong, *Korean Folk Painting*, Emile Museum 1977.

Index

Please email Valmik Thapar
at tiger@vsnl.com
if you have any information
or pictures on the tiger's cult.